BRIDGING THE COMMUNICATION GAP

Since the dawn of history, human beings and dogs have been friends and companions, each adding something very precious to the other's life. You and your dog are part of the great tradition.

Yet between your desire to love your dog and his desire to have you as a master there exists an element that can destroy your relationship. Quite simply it is a gap in communication.

This book is a work to bring you and your dog together—an essential guide for everyone who owns a dog.
"A badly behaved dog is a display of bad manners by the dog's owner. Mordecai Siegal and Matthew Margolis have written the book that will correct both dog and owner most easily, surely and humanely."—Roger Caras

MORDECAI SIEGAL writes a monthly column for *House Beautiful*. He is a contributing editor to *Pure-Bred Dogs—American Kennel Gazette* (AKC) and *Dogs Magazine*. He is the author of *The Good Dog Book*.

MATTHEW MARGOLIS is the founder of the National Institute of Dog Training, Inc., and has trained over 5,000 dogs (and their owners) in their own homes.

GOOD DOG, BAD DOG

MORDECAI SIEGAL

&

MATTHEW MARGOLIS

A SIGNET BOOK

SIGNET
Published by the Penguin Group
Penguin Books USA Inc., 375 Hudson Street,
New York, New York 10014, U.S.A.
Penguin Books Ltd, 27 Wrights Lane,
London W8 5TZ, England
Penguin Books Australia Ltd, Ringwood,
Victoria, Australia
Penguin Books Canada Ltd, 2801 John Street,
Markham, Ontario, Canada L3R 1B4
Penguin Books (N.Z.) Ltd, 182–190 Wairau Road,
Auckland 10, New Zealand

Penguin Books Ltd, Registered Offices:
Harmondsworth, Middlesex, England

Published by Signet, an imprint of New American Library, a division of
Penguin Books USA Inc.

This is an authorized reprint of a hardcover edition published by Holt,
Rinehart and Winston, Inc. The hardcover edition was published simultaneously
in Canada by Holt, Rinehart and Winston of Canada, Limited.

First Printing, October, 1974
25   24   23   22   21   20   19   18

Drawings by Marion Krupp

 REGISTERED TRADEMARK—MARCA REGISTRADA

Printed in the United States of America

For
Pete, Princess, and Silver . . .

Three Lucky Dogs

Contents

The authors wish to express their gratitude and appreciation to Mark Handler for his skill and sensitivity as photographer for *Good Dog, Bad Dog*.

To Beverly Margolis and Vicki Siegal a special note of admiration for their patience and assistance.

A special thank you to Don Gold and Hy Shore for the application of their very special gifts to this book.

Introduction

> If you pick up a starving dog and make him prosperous, he will not bite you. This is the principal difference between a dog and a man.
>
> —MARK TWAIN

Now that the commitment has been made to own a dog, it is reasonable to want to know how to take care of him. After all, these bundles of fur are totally dependent creatures and innocently look to their owners for food, shelter, medical attention, and love. Everything connected with their survival depends on the big guys, the humans. And in the human world a dog's survival often hinges on his ability to respond to a direct command. "Pete, stay!" "Silver, come!" "No!" "Down!" "Sit!" These are not arbitrary orders shouted from the Gestapo Handbook. They are scientific commands given to a trained animal whose correct response may save his life in city traffic or rural hazards. These commands will also allow for a satisfying relationship between dog and master. If a dog is not housebroken, not able to be silent, not able to keep from destroying furniture or property, not able to obey when required, then his survival is in jeopardy. Many people give up their dogs after a few months of abject frustration, and the future of those animals is then in grave danger. This is why obedience training is not only valuable but necessary.

With the many books available concerning dog training, one might ask what's special about this one. To begin with, the premise of this book is that the owner is being trained how to train his or her dog. Equal emphasis is given to teaching the owner as well as the animal.

As owner-operator of the National Institute of Dog Training, Inc., coauthor Matthew Margolis has trained approximately five thousand dogs *and their owners* in their homes. He is one of the pioneers in the techniques of owner-animal training in the home. The benefits of his experience are herewith offered.

This is the first dog-training book that attempts to dig beneath the surface of its own method and explain how the technique works. Within these pages are offered a basic obedience training course that has proven itself over and over with thousands of dogs of all breeds. No training book has ever gone beneath the surface to understand the behavioral characteristics of specific breeds and how to use that understanding in training. This one does. It is the first practical guide to training your dog *at home*. It emphasizes affection, kindness, and authority. It is based on the idea that dogs are nice.

PART 1

The Basic Obedience Course

1/Success

GOOD DOG, GOOD OWNER

Being a dog is a boring job. Most of his life is spent either sleeping or waiting to be fed. Chances are the dog is bored beyond belief. This is especially true if his owner does not know how to communicate with him, to convey what is wanted, or to spend the necessary time relating so that a rapport exists. Dogs are in a foreign country and do not understand the language. Which may explain why they seek the company of other dogs. Most dog owners are kind and generous people. They need only to develop consistent goals and principles to enjoy the many years of companionship and protection that a dog gives.

The difference between a good dog and a bad dog is whether or not he makes his owner feel like a benevolent master who is always in control. As lord of the manor, it is the owner's noble obligation to offer shelter, hearty nutrition, proper medical attention, exercise, affection, and training. In return the dog should respond with love, joy, undying devotion, and *absolute* obedience. Although it seems a bit medieval, this is approximately the ideal dog-master relationship. Successful training helps achieve this goal. This course deals exclusively with obedience because it has been proven through experience that the entire dog-master relationship improves greatly after an effective training course.

THE PROPER FRAME OF MIND

To successfully train a dog, the owner must maintain the cool objectivity of a "pro." This means not allowing frustrations to interfere with relating to the dog. Many mistakes are going to be made by the dog as he proceeds from lesson to lesson throughout the course, and the owner's patience will be put to the test over and over again. The dog must not be yelléd at or punished in any way. If the owner has had a trying day he must either postpone the lesson or stay alert not to abuse the dog because he didn't get that promotion, or his wife dented a fender, or his teen-age daughter moved into a co-educational dorm. One must exercise patience, kindness, and an understanding of emotional limitations and personal inadequacies. Many a kicked dog has been a stand-in for the boss, the wife, the husband, the mother-in-law. Before expressing anger at the dog, ask if he really deserves it. There is no place in this obedience course for abuses. Forget the word *punishment*. Replace it with the word *correction*.

WHY TRAIN A DOG?

The answer to this question has to do with why one buys a dog at all. There are many reasons why people keep dogs. Pleasure, companionship, protection, child education are a few, but mainly it's to enjoy the animal. No living being will love you as completely as a dog. Training will at once remove the obstacles standing between the owner and the beneficial objectives of dog ownership, thus allowing many trouble-free years with the animal.

Without training, cute puppy behavior soon develops into annoying adult habits. These annoying habits sometimes become severe problems and permanently damage the dog's temperament. But with a trained dog you will never have to cope with dog fighting, being dragged down the street, being jumped on, or having furniture destroyed. Obedience training also eliminates stealing food from the table, defecating indoors, throwing up in the car, or the hundreds of other problems that make it unpleasant to own an animal. If a dog does any combination of these things he is not a bad dog. He is merely untrained. This is a correctable situation; it is well within the owner's grasp to change it.

Dogs are like babies, and as there is no such thing as a bad baby, there is no such thing as a bad puppy. Dogs are shaped by environmental influences as well as the genetic characteristics of the dog's bloodline. If a dog is trained properly he will behave like a gentleman and cause very few problems throughout his life. A good definition of training is *teaching a dog to respond to his master and doing what is expected of him the minute a command is given.* Any dog can be trained and any owner can train him.

DISPELLING MYTHS FROM THE DARK AGES

It is important to forget the hearsay methods of dog training that have been handed down through the ages like snake oil in a medicine show. Chances are it was Attila the Hun who first rubbed his dog's nose in his own mess and yelled and screamed at him. Forget that "method." Forget all methods that brutalize and are abusive, such as swatting with a rolled-up newspaper. It teaches the dog nothing except to fear long cylindrical objects (including your hands) and to run when he sees them. It is merely another form of punishment, and that accomplishes nothing positive beyond giving you emotional release.

Do you hit your dog? Of course not. But some confused, frustrated owners do. A flinching, cowering, neurotic animal is a giveaway. The owner says in protest ". . . but I really love Tinkle. I only kicked her because she was a bad dog." This obedience course shows a better way to make a dog behave and replaces antiquated techniques. Forever resolve not to hit, kick, pinch, punch, gouge, slap, knuckle, tweak, bang, strike, nip, or bite your dog. Please refrain from ever using your hand for anything other than hand signals (used in giving commands) or affectionate praise or love. Never use your hand for threats, violent gestures, or even disciplinary pointing. Pointing your finger at the dog and saying "Naughty, naughty" produces the same negative effect. Pain, fear, and terror retard or prohibit communication. It is also inhumane.

Imagine entering a taxi in a foreign country. The driver asks "Where to?" in his native tongue. You stare at him and shrug, not knowing the language. He then goes berserk and smacks you hard on the snout. It would seem painfully unreasonable, to say the least. Some dogs face this horror every day of their lives. If hitting a dog was the least bit useful, why would it have to be done so often? Your dog can be trained with absolute results without being punished. This is an opportunity to stop feeling guilty by giving your dog a punishment-free life. This will enable you to enjoy your friend, the dog.

WHEN TO BEGIN TRAINING

Training can begin at age three months for puppies of all breeds. By this we mean housebreaking (or paper training), the command "Heel" (to the extent of getting the puppy used to the leash), and the command "Sit." At age four and a half months the entire course may be taught.

WHO SHOULD PARTICIPATE IN THE TRAINING

Ideally, every member of the family should learn the new techniques in order to avoid confusing the dog. For obvious reasons, only one person should introduce the training to the animal. After the dog has learned each new command, the instructor then teaches the rest of the family what to do and how to do it. If everyone participated in the training at the same time, it would become more of a chaotic party than a lesson for the dog and the session would go out the window. What with cross-conversations, inconsistent commands, and the general tumult, the dog's attentiveness would disappear.

It is best to teach the dog a command with no one else around. It may take from one to three sessions for him to respond immediately to the new command. Once he does, do not turn him over to the rest of the family until he has had time to rest and absorb what he has learned. Give him at least five hours before showing the other members of the family. Then take them one at a time and teach them how to execute the new command. This will give you the responsibility of correcting them with patience.

THE BASIC OBEDIENCE COURSE

No training session should last longer than fifteen minutes. Dogs tire and bore very easily. If you work a dog more than fifteen minutes he is going to respond to every distraction imaginable. Try to be extra patient and understanding during the first few sessions. He is going to be denied every impulse that is natural for him. It will be a whole new world of discipline and obedience. You are going to create conditioned responses in his brain that will make it impossible for him to disregard a command. This represents a major mental chore for the dog and will make him moody and irritable when the first sessions are over Allow for this by letting him sleep after the sessions. Sleep is probably what he'll want.

These minor considerations for the animal come out of your understanding his immediate problems. Every chapter will contain a section entitled "Beneath the Surface of the Training." With every new command, this section will explain the natural instinct of the dog and how you are going to change or manipulate that instinct. The result should be a greater understanding of the dog in relation to the command. It is important, however, to attempt to analyze your own dog. He is a *student* and like all students has his positive and negative qualities. Every dog has a different personality. How does *your* dog react in certain situations?

The best way to train your dog is to utilize his good attributes. If he is very affectionate then that should be the key to getting a good response from him. He will respond to the giving or withholding of affection. With other dogs too much affection will not bring good results. He may assume that every time you praise him he can then revert back to doing as he pleases. In other circumstances a withdrawn dog will possibly respond better to praise and affection. Determine if your dog is affectionate, stubborn, spiteful, outgoing, withdrawn, afraid of noises, etc. Of course it is safe to assume that a three-month-old puppy is going to be playful, outgoing, energetic, and generally responsive to affection. They often make the best students.

Pick a suitable area where the training is to be given. Inside the home is fine, providing there is ample walking space and a minimum of distractions. Outdoors, a quiet, secluded area is best. It is futile to teach a command such as "Sit" when there are eight dogs in heat hanging around, plus an airplane crash, and ten young boys playing baseball.

Communication is the prime factor in training a dog. He does not speak or understand English. His intelligence level is that of a small child. Therefore you must seek his level of understanding. He will respond mostly to a tone of voice. Like an actor, you must pretend firmness, softness, or play-fulness through vocal tone and attitude. If you have ever communicated with an infant you will understand what is meant here. It's almost the same thing. "Goo-goo" makes a baby smile. A firmly said "No" makes him let go of your glasses. Once you have established lines of communication you are halfway finished with the training.

2 / Equipment

There are enough manufactured dog items to completely fill a supermarket—more than one could use in a lifetime. If you bought them all you could create a do-it-yourself Spanish Inquisition. Cattle prods, throw-chains, and various electrical gadgets would be more suitable for counter-intelligence interrogations. Very few, however, are useful for training purposes.

A great hindrance to acquiring practical training equipment is the "rhinestone and paisley" syndrome. Several years ago a Park Avenue client contracted for an obedience course for her dog. Her silver-gray poodle was about as clipped and manicured as they came. When the rather grand lady was asked for the dog's training equipment, she opened a closet door and revealed over fifty collars and leashes of every color, style, and description. She became self-conscious after the trainer gasped. She explained that she always bought Pipa a new collar and leash whenever she purchased a new clothing ensemble for herself. She and her Pipa were at all times fashion coordinated. However, she did not have the very few items necessary to properly control the dog. Unless one is interested in making "Best-Dressed Dog of the Year," there are few items needed to train a dog.

THINGS THAT *WON'T* BE NEEDED

A spiked collar. A spiked or pronged collar is a choke collar with bent prongs on the underside, the ends of which dig into the animal's neck when pulled on its slip device. These prongs, though blunted, make dozens of tiny impressions around the throat and effectively restrict the dog's movement when jerked into operation. It is true that they can be useful when used properly by a professional trainer, but the chance of misusing it and seriously injuring your dog is great. One jerk with a pronged collar is worth fifteen jerks with a regular choke collar. However, inexperienced dog owners tend to overdo it and make the animal suffer or become permanently damaged.

A leash made of chain. No matter how long or short, it is almost impossible to tell ahead of time when it is going to snap. If it should break while in city traffic the dog might bolt, run out in the street, and the rest is too unpleasant to think about. One can see where a leather leash is wearing thin or losing its stitching.

Thick, short leashes. They are useless for training purposes. They may look very masculine with a Doberman or Shepherd on the end of them, but they are very ineffective for employing the various training techniques that will be discussed in the coming chapters.

Leather collars. For reasons that will become clear, they work against the training technique. The exceptions to this are the long-haired breeds such as Afghans, Sheepdogs, etc. In that situation a leather collar is preferable because a metal one tends to rub the fur away and create permanent ring marks or bald spots.

THINGS THAT *WILL* BE NEEDED

A six-foot leather leash. This is used in every command except where otherwise indicated. It will allow the proper distance for control when teaching the dog to "Sit." Six feet of leash will also allow you to walk behind him while still exercising control. A leather leash, by the way, will not hurt your hand or the dog's chest when employing various training techniques.

Leashes come in various widths. The size of your dog should guide you in choosing the proper width, although five-eighths of an inch is recommended as the most comfortable width without sacrificing strength. Toy breeds require a narrower width such as the half-inch or smaller. The key to buying this equipment is strength and comfort. A fancy, multicolored nylon leash may look beautiful but might break and then you won't have a dog.

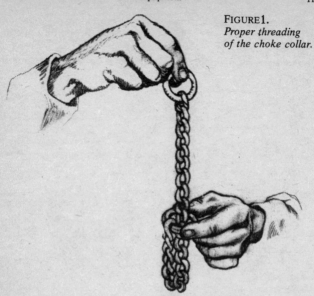

FIGURE 1.
*Proper threading
of the choke collar.*

A twenty-five-foot clothesline. Used as a long leash, this rope is implemented when teaching "Sit-Stay" *off-leash.*

A fifty-foot clothesline. This length of rope is employed as a leash when teaching the dog to "Come When Called" *off-leash.*

A jeweled choke collar. A jeweled choke collar is one that has small metal links which are welded very close together. This type is the strongest and releases its grip from the dog's neck quickly and smoothly. The wide-linked choke collars sometimes jam as one link entangles in another. For correct threading of the jeweled choke collar, see Figure 1. The term "choke" collar is a misnomer. It does not choke the dog. It "corrects" the dog by tightening around his neck when the leash is pulled. If the collar is placed around the dog's neck properly it will release quickly, thus avoiding any pain. (See Fig. 2). *Do not use a metal choke collar for Toy breeds and small puppies.* These dogs are too fragile for this equipment. Either use a leather collar or slip the end of a nylon leash through the hand loop, thus effecting a slip knot around the animal's neck.

FIGURE 2.
*Left: correct way for dog to
wear the choke collar.
Right: incorrect way.*

A *"throw can."* This is another misnomer. It is not really
used for throwing. Similar to a New Year's Eve noisemaker,
it is used to startle a dog and get his immediate attention.
Take an empty soda can and slip fifteen pennies into it, taping
the opening closed. By rattling it up and down you get a demanding sound. This is used primarily for puppy problems
such as housebreaking, chewing, jumping, going into the
garbage, chasing the baby, etc. Shake the can and say "No"
in a firm voice. The noise becomes associated with the word
"No" and stops the puppy from continuing his indiscretion.

This is all the equipment one needs to successfully complete the obedience course. The outlay of money is nominal.

These items are standard and available in any pet supply outlet. Please resist the temptation to substitute these items with homemade, inadequate versions or storebought, overly complex versions of the same things. Purchase exactly what is suggested. This equipment is uncomplicated, inexpensive, and highly functional. Once the equipment is procured you are ready to begin the course. Good luck.

3 / Housebreaking

One of the great agonies for dog owners is housebreaking. Here is a method to solve that problem. There are many reasons why a dog is not housebroken, but the prime cause is the inability to communicate what is wanted from him. Most new dog owners are extremely inhibited and embarrassed by the whole subject of housebreaking. If dealing with the functions of the animal body is too embarrassing, how then can one teach the animal to control those functions? Many dog owners behave like six-year-old children making "toidy" jokes in a Gilbert and Sullivan operetta. "Muff-Muff make do-do." "Princess made ta-ta." Nothing is worse than hearing a grown person say of his 185-pound Mastiff, "Horace makes tinkle on the bed." The worst ever recorded was, "Poofie makes chocolates in the house!" It is desirable to avoid such euphemisms as *surprises, plops, wee-wee, ca-ca, eh-eh, gifts*(!), *presents, numbers one and two, feces, movements, etc.* A dog defecates. A dog urinates. Let's be brave about it.

DEFINITION OF HOUSEBREAKING

It is simply, teaching your dog to relieve himself, outside, on a schedule most convenient for you.

BENEATH THE SURFACE
OF THE TRAINING

There is no such thing as a partly housebroken dog. Many an owner has said something like, "Fang is completely housebroken . . . except he dumps on the bed after we change the linen." Either he is housebroken or he isn't. Some people say their dog is housebroken when they mean he's paper-trained. There is a considerable difference between the two. When a dog is housebroken he never, but *never,* uses the house for his toilet, on or off the newspaper.

Many people do not understand why their dog does not know what to do when taken outside. Merely taking him outside does not mean that he knows what he's being taken out for. The biggest problem between dog and owner is that the dog would love to please but doesn't know how; and the owner would love to teach the dog what he wants but doesn't know how to communicate to the dog. This method solves that problem. There is nothing worse than a dog who is not housebroken. It is the first and most important phase of domesticating an animal. Many a dog and owner have parted company at this phase of their relationship. Many a good and loving dog has been saved from being given away or destroyed after the owner was introduced to this housebreaking method.

PROCEDURE AND TECHNIQUE FOR HOUSEBREAKING

This technique is the most humane ever devised. With it there is no confusion for the animal. Each phase has its importance and each phase should be followed the way it is outlined. There are four major steps:

1. Proper diet and scheduling
2. Using an odor neutralizer
3. Confining the dog
4. Proper correction (not punishment)

This method is ideal for dogs between three months and three years old. However, good results have been gotten with dogs as old as six years. Of course you will not get the same results with a six-year-old as with a puppy, but the method does work. The ideal age to start housebreaking your dog is when he is approximately twelve weeks old. By that time one assumes he has visited a veterinarian and has had his permanent shots and there is no chance of his catching distemper, leptospirosis, or canine hepatitis. The method should take no more than two to four weeks. You should find a great improvement in the first week. If the dog does not respond, it is possible that he has a medical problem and should be examined by a veterinarian. If you have been paper training your dog, pick up the papers and forget that technique. Otherwise the animal will become totally confused.

PROPER DIET AND SCHEDULING

Feed, water, and walk your dog properly. He needs a stable, well-balanced diet consisting of correct amounts of fat, proteins, carbohydrates, vitamins, and minerals. The ideal dog food is pure meat added to some form of cereal. Canned meat products mixed with commercial cereal are adequate. Commercial dog food has all the vitamins and minerals essential for your dog's well-being and it is recommended. Table scraps are a hit-or-miss affair. When changing the dog's diet, do not do it all at once. Gradually mix the two diets over a three-day period so that the change is not sudden. Otherwise it will cause diarrhea. A dog's stomach is very sensitive to changes of food.

Feed, water, and walk the dog at the same times each day to achieve favorable results. Consistency is the key to this method. The following rules must be followed without variance:

1. Do not vary your dog's diet.
2. Snacks or between-meal treats are forbidden.

Putting your dog on a proper schedule. Here is the ideal schedule for a three- to five-month-old puppy (follow the established diet pattern for older dogs): seven-thirty in the morning—feed, water, and walk him; eleven-thirty in the morning—feed, water, and walk him; four-thirty in the afternoon—feed, water, and walk him; eight-thirty in the evening—water only and a walk; eleven-thirty in the evening—just a walk.

At feed time allow fifteen minutes for the dog to complete his meal and then take it away, no matter how much he has left in the bowl. Allow him a few minutes to drink water. *He is not to be given food except at the scheduled times.* (This dietary schedule is for the duration of the housebreaking period only.) Water should be made available at all times.

Please consult a veterinarian on all matters pertaining to your dog's diet.

The more one restricts the time for food and water, the closer one comes to scheduling the dog's bodily functions. A dish with four or five ice cubes may substitute for a bowl of water, thus satisfying the dog's thirst while reducing his water intake. Once again we advise you to consult a veterinarian about the specific needs of your dog.

The minute the dog is fed and watered, take him out for his walk. Once he has relieved himself, praise him and take him inside immediately. He will soon begin to understand why he is being taken out.

The length of time a dog should be walked must not exceed fifteen or twenty minutes. If taken on a long walk before or after he has performed his bodily functions the impact of *why* he is being taken out will have been diminished and the method will not work. This is exactly why most dogs do not know what is expected of them when they are taken outside.

Schedule for nine-to-five working people. Take the dog out immediately after waking up. Bring him back inside, feed and water him, and then walk him once again so that the routine is established. When you come home from work repeat the process. Take him out, back in for feeding and watering, and then out for another immediate walking. It would be good for the dog if you could arrange for someone to repeat this cycle at lunchtime. Before going to bed walk him one last time without a feeding. Because a small puppy cannot hold his water for eight or nine hours, it is advisable to confine him to an area that he can urinate in without causing any household damage.

If the dog has a favorite outdoor area let him go there to sniff around. Many dogs develop a favorite spot and it should not be discouraged.

When this program is first begun, do not be frustrated if the dog does not relieve himself for the first two or three rounds of feeding, watering, and walking. He may hold out for as long as twenty hours. Bear in mind that he is being forced to break his old habits and do something new for the first time. If he holds out for too long, then insert a glycerin baby suppository in his anus after his feeding and watering. Take him outside. You will get results. After he relieves himself, praise him so that he knows that going outside pleases you. All this is temporary until the dog is housebroken.

USING AN ODOR NEUTRALIZER

The second phase of housebreaking, and probably the most important, is getting rid of the dog's past urinary and excretory odors from the house. This is accomplished with an odor neutralizer, which is available in pet stores and pharmacies. When used properly it will completely eliminate these odors, sometimes discerned only by the dog, by neutralizing them rather than perfuming or covering them with a stronger scent. Place twenty drops of the liquid neutralizer into three quarts of hot water. With this mixture mop all areas where the dog has messed. If all such areas are neutralized, dogs will relieve themselves indoors less frequently. When your dog has to relieve himself he seeks an area where he or another dog has gone. This can be borne out by observing him outdoors. He sniffs around for a very specific spot before he performs.

It is important to note that no ordinary cleaning product neutralizes these odors. Ammonia, bleach, and detergents of every kind fail for one reason. They are not designed for this purpose. Consequently, the dog's odor remains long after the mess has been cleaned away. A liquid odor neutralizer does its job every time. If your dog urinates in the house, your first step toward success is to odor-neutralize the spot frequently. This process should be repeated each and every time the dog has an accident in order to prevent him from returning to the scene of the crime.

CONFINING THE DOG

The third phase of housebreaking is *watching* and *confining* the dog. For whatever the reason, there are many times when the dog must be left alone in the house. This, very often, is precisely when he chooses to relieve himself. It is rare that he will attempt it before your eyes after the first experience with your scorn. Therefore, confine the dog when he is left alone. Confinement, however, does not mean tying him up. He is simply contained in a small area where he cannot stray. Psychologically, a dog will never defecate in an area where he must remain. His habit is to go as far away as possible, relieve himself, and then go back to his own area. The area of confinement must be large enough for him to walk around without feeling punished. Otherwise, he'll bark and try to get out.

When you are home the dog should be allowed to run around loose, *providing you watch him*. If he is going to relieve himself, be in a position to correct him immediately. The key to watching and confining is that the dog will not mess in his own area if he can help it. However, if he is never let loose to run around the house it becomes too much like punishment, and that will work against this method.

PROPER CORRECTION

The final phase of housebreaking is the technique for correction. Under no circumstances should a dog be punished for relieving himself in the house. He cannot be justifiably punished for his ignorance; he can only be corrected.

Never correct a dog unless you catch him in the act. A few minutes after the deed has been done, the dog has no mental capacity to connect your wrath with whatever he did wrong. It is confusing to him and you will only get a puzzled whimper. That's why punishments have little or no effect and only lead to frustration for dog and owner. Catch him in the act or it's no good.

When the dog messes in the house in front of you, there is only one way to correct him. Do not rub his face in it. Do not say "shame." Do not play negative games with the newspaper or other threatening objects. *Startle* and *impress* him with the word "No." This is where you use the "throw can." (See Chapter 2.) When the dog is in the act of urinating, shake the can vigorously like a party noisemaker. This should be accompanied with a harsh "No." Whatever he is doing, he will probably stop. When he does, immediately take him outside to finish what he started. *This is the only way that you can show the dog what you want him to do.* You are catching him in the act, stopping him, taking him outside to finish, and then giving him tremendous praise when he finishes.

The difference between shaking the can and slapping a newspaper in your hand is the difference between getting his attention or threatening him with a slap or blow. Do not instill fear in the animal. Stop him in the middle of his action so that he can be taken to the proper place for it. The correction really comes from the harsh "No." With a large dog it may be necessary to throw the can on the floor (behind your back, preferably) to stop him. During this period, if necessary, leave the leash and collar on so that he can be taken outside quickly with no delay. The idea is to correct, not punish.

Many people are mistakenly convinced that dogs mess in the house for spite or revenge, usually for having been left alone. This is incorrect. It is for reasons of anxiety, nervousness, or fear that he behaves this way . . . or simply because he is not properly housebroken. Very often an owner comes home and finds the dog behaving in a fearful, shameful, or generally guilt-ridden manner. The owner knows the dog has messed somewhere. It is because of this behavior that an owner is convinced the dog messes in the house for spite. It simply isn't true. The dog cringes when you come home because he associates your arrival with punishment. He does not understand what he has done wrong in the specific sense. If the dog is left alone in a new place or in a situation that makes him nervous or frightened, he will uncontrollably defecate. It has nothing to do with his ability to perform as a well-behaved, housebroken pet.

Many methods of housebreaking are negative in approach. Consequently, the dog half understands. He knows he's done something wrong. But he gets little or no instruction for what he should be doing. The first emphasis of this method is prevention and the second is instruction. This was once illustrated to a client who called the trainer at home at three in the morning after he had been asleep for several hours. A frantic voice asked, "Mr. Margolis?"

"Yes," he mumbled.

"This is Mrs. Baxter. You're training my little Filbert."

"Yes," he answered, "but it's three in the morning. What do you want?"

"You told me to call you if Filbert had an accident. Well he made do-do on the rug. What should I do?"

"Clean it up," he said as he hung up the phone. That's instruction.

4 / Paper Training

In the world of dogs, pouring over the Sunday papers has an entirely different connotation. Next to reporting the news, the greatest service rendered to the public by newspapers is to provide an inexhaustible supply of paper-training equipment. Paper training is an ideal alternative to housebreaking for many reasons. The convenience of not having to use the streets at all hours of the day and night speaks for itself. Inclement weather and rigorous work schedules are also good reasons for wanting to stay off the streets. But possibly the best reason of all is one that most city dwellers are familiar with. That is, the aesthetic problem involved in soiling the city streets and sidewalks with dog litter.

In large urban areas such as New York City, where over six hundred thousand dogs reside, many nondog owners have created a major public issue of this subject and have lobbied for restrictive legislation against dogs and dog owners. The authors do not believe that legislation is an effective answer to this problem. However, paper training offers an excellent alternative to this irksome situation. If paper training were adopted by enough considerate dog owners it would mean the end of one more aspect of the pollution problem in American cities. For those who love their dogs but are also concerned with ecology, the end of the conflict lies in paper training.

DEFINITION OF PAPER TRAINING

This means that a dog will urinate and defecate on paper in your house or apartment, in a designated area of your choice.

BENEATH THE SURFACE
OF THE TRAINING

The main reason a dog prefers to urinate on paper is because the urine disappears by absorption. That you remove the papers after he uses them is soon understood. No animal wants to be around his own body waste. Another reason why paper training works so well is that dogs prefer to toilet on the same spot they did previously. It has to do with the territorial instinct for claiming specific areas as their own. Because of a dog's highly developed sense of smell, he is capable of detecting scents of which we are completely unaware. Consequently, after he has soiled one spot he is drawn back to the same place simply because he can smell it. Only a powerful odor neutralizer can prevent his smelling it.

Paper training is most successful when introduced to the animal as a puppy. If the choice is made to paper train, you must not change over to housebreaking. Too often a pup is taken away from his litter before ten weeks and cannot be taken outside for housebreaking. The owner uses newspapers, indoors, as a temporary measure. It is a mistake to then take the puppy away from his paper procedure. This offers nothing but confusion to the little dog. As a result the dog starts having one accident after another in his attempt to interpret your wishes. These accidents often occur on an expensive carpet or in a corner of your bedroom during the night. The dog is then punished or shamed or burdened with unjust guilt while the owner suffers from frustration and rage. This is also the beginning of neurotic behavior in most animals.

The rule should be that you do not take a puppy into your house before he is ten weeks old unless you are firm in your resolution to paper train him. In the case of dogs that have already been housebroken, it is only fair to say that the changeover will be difficult and will demand a great deal of patience.

PROCEDURE AND TECHNIQUE
FOR PAPER TRAINING

There are four steps to paper training:

1. Proper diet and scheduling

2. Confining the dog
3. Using an odor neutralizer
4. Proper correction

These steps are primarily geared for puppies, although they can be used for older dogs if you take a little more time and exercise greater patience. What should be done first is to pick an area in the house that is convenient for this purpose. Designate it as the permanent paper place for the dog. Here is where he will always relieve himself and feel confident that you will not be angry when he uses it. This will be where you *paper* the dog. Some of the more convenient places to use are the bathroom, the kitchen, the pantry, the basement, or any place where you're least likely to be offended when the dog uses it. Do not, however, pick a place that is inaccessible for him. The easier it is for him to get there the more success you will have.

PROPER DIET AND SCHEDULING

Feed, water, and paper the dog properly. He needs a stable, well-balanced diet consisting of correct amounts of fat, protein, carbohydrates, vitamins, and minerals. As discussed in the housebreaking chapter, the ideal dog food is pure meat mixed with some form of cereal. It is not advisable to make sudden dietary changes. Because of intestinal sensitivity, this will cause diarrhea. First, consult a veterinarian for the nutritional needs of your dog. Then, combine the new food mixture with the old one. Phase the old one out over a three-day period.

Feed, water, and walk the dog at the same times each day to achieve favorable results. Consistency is the key to this method. By timing an animal's intake of food you can determine when he will relieve himself. It usually takes food from six to eight hours to pass through his system.

Putting your dog on a proper schedule. The dog must be given the opportunity to use the paper a minimum of four times a day. He is to be fed, watered, and papered—*in that order.*
Here is the ideal schedule for a three- to five-month-old puppy (follow the established diet pattern for older dogs):

seven-thirty in the morning—feed, water, and paper; eleven-thirty in the morning—feed, water, and paper; four-thirty in the afternoon—feed, water, and paper; eight-thirty in the evening—water only and paper; eleven-thirty in the evening—just the paper.

At feeding time allow fifteen minutes for the dog to complete his meal and then take it away, no matter how much he has left in the bowl. He is not to be given food except at the scheduled times. Keep an ample supply of water available at all times. A dish of ice cubes will limit the dog's water intake yet quench his thirst. The more you restrict the time for food and water the closer you come to scheduling his bodily functions.

The minute the dog is fed and watered he is to be allowed to use the paper. Praise him each time he urinates or defecates on the paper and then remove him to another room. He will quickly understand what the paper is for.

Schedule for nine-to-five working people. Take the dog to the paper immediately after waking up. Allow him to use it. Once he does, you may immediately feed, water, and then paper him once again so that the routine is established. He is then to be confined in one area (outlined in greater detail later in this chapter) with the newspaper laid out for him. You are now able to leave the house for work. On coming home, repeat the process: feed, water, and paper. Before bedtime place him on the paper one last time without a feeding or watering. Because a small puppy cannot hold his water for eight or nine hours, it is advisable not to give him the run of the house. Confine him to one small area.

The length of time a dog is allowed to use the paper should not exceed ten minutes. If he hasn't performed in that time chances are he's not going to and he should be removed. Sometimes sprinkling a little water on the paper encourages him to use it. An effective technique is to save one sheet of previously soiled paper to place underneath the new sheets. The smell will give him the idea of what is wanted. When first beginning this program do not be frustrated if the dog does not relieve himself for the first two or three rounds of feeding, watering, and papering. He may hold out for as long as twenty hours, especially in the case of older dogs. If your patience wears thin you may use a glycerin baby suppository. Insert it in the dog's anus after his feeding and watering. Although a bit indelicate, it produces the desired result. After he relieves himself give him a great deal of praise so that he knows that using the paper pleases you. That is essentially what he wants to do.

CONFINING THE DOG

From the first moment you start this program, after selecting the proper place, lay newspaper over the entire room in a three- to five-sheet thickness. Do not miss a spot. This must be done for the first five days. If the dog is placed on an area that is completely covered with paper he has no choice but to do the right thing. Immediately after he uses the paper pick it up, but save one sheet that is soiled and place it underneath the fresh sheets the next time around. If the dog is a very young puppy he may use the paper nine or ten times a day. He will sniff, circle around, or let you know in some way that he wants to use the paper. Learn his signals. As he gets older he will go at less frequent intervals.

After the fifth day, start narrowing down the amount of space you cover with the newspaper. Pick up the soiled paper but replace it with less and less paper, until after several days you are laying down only as much paper as he needs. By this time he will probably have confined himself to one favored spot in the room. Of course, if in the first five days you notice that he has already started using one small area then that is the time to start using less paper. In any event, this process should not take more than two days after the first five days of totally covering the room with paper.

Every pet owner is sooner or later faced with the problem of leaving the untrained dog alone. It is a nagging dilemma for any pet owner, but more so for the novice. One usually comes home to a house littered with urine and fecal matter. If the dog has ever been yelled at for his indiscretions he will wait until left alone to do his worst. This is why confining the dog is important. Do not misinterpret this to mean that you should tie the dog down. Select a small, convenient area where the dog cannot stray and confine him in it. *This area must be where he uses his papers.* It is extremely unpleasant for a dog to relieve himself in the same area where he must remain. It is for this reason that confinement acts as an aid in this training. The area of confinement must not be so restrictive that the animal has no room to walk around. That would be like punishment and cause him to bark and try to escape the confinement. If his papers are available he'll use them and walk to the other portion of his area. This too helps the training process.

To avoid making the puppy's life oppressive, allow him to run around loose when you are home. This is desirable *providing you watch him.* Always be prepared to correct him if he begins to relieve himself off the papers. If he is never let loose to run around the house it becomes too much like punishment, and that will work against this training method.

USING AN ODOR NEUTRALIZER

When the dog makes a mistake and relieves himself in the house in a place that is not covered with newspaper, there are two things that must be done. First, there is the correction which will be dealt with in "Proper Correction," which follows. The second thing is to get rid of the odor quickly. This is important. Even when the spot is washed the smell is discernible to the animal. That is why ordinary cleaning products are useless for this purpose. Ammonia, bleach, detergents, and various household sprays do not work. Only a strong liquid odor neutralizer actually eliminates the scent. Place twenty drops of neutralizer into three quarts of hot water. Mop all soiled areas with this mixture.

A dog cannot help himself once he gets the scent of his own urine or defecation. Even though we cannot smell it ourselves, he does, and is inevitably drawn to it. Dogs mark their territory by urinating on key parts of it. Other dogs come along and mark the same spot. When walking your dog you can observe that he is smelling for his or another dog's odor. That is why you should neutralize the odor of all indoor areas where the dog has relieved himself. By removing the scent of his own waste matter you will prevent him from repeating his indiscretion on the same spot.

PROPER CORRECTION

Under no circumstances should a dog be punished for relieving himself off the paper. He can only be corrected. *Unless you are actually there to stop the dog as he begins to relieve himself, it is useless to correct him.* Punishments, indeed, not even mild corrections, have any effect in the dog's mind if a few minutes have elapsed between his act and your correction. His mental processes are quite limited in this respect.

This brings us to the meaning of "correction" as the word is used throughout this training program. To *correct* the animal is to communicate to him that he has displeased you. In paper training, as in housebreaking, the technique of correction involves use of the word "No," which must be said in a firm tone of voice. The objective is to startle the dog and thereby impress upon him your displeasure. However, this can only be communicated to him if he is in the middle of his wrongdoing. If one's voice is too mild or if the dog does not respond to the firm "No," it can be accompanied with the noise of the "throw can." (See Chapter 2.)

As the dog relieves himself off the papers rattle the pennies inside the can vigorously and simultaneously say, "No," firmly. That much noise will have to stop the dog. It is precisely at that moment that he should be taken to his papers. Praise him for having stopped what he was doing at your command. Allow him to finish his act, on the papers. Then once again give him a great deal of praise. *This is the only way that you can show the dog what to do.* It is, quite literally, a teaching process.

Paper training, like housebreaking, should not be approached from a negative perspective. If it is, the dog will only understand half the training. He will understand that he has displeased you, but he must be made to understand what to do so that you will be pleased with him. Communicating to him what you expect is the objective of all dog training. Keeping the dog off the carpets and the city streets is the objective of paper training.

5 / Proper Use of "No" and "Okay"

Spoken words are vocalized symbols that are used to communicate information, emotion, or combinations of the two. But for the purposes of dog training, words are used as tools for manipulating behavior. In this context we weigh our words carefully when training a dog to submit to our will. Two very valuable words are "No" and "Okay." These tools should not be used in a wasteful and unproductive manner. To wit, "Sidney, *no,* get your head out of the garbage." Or, "*Okay,* Sidney, what did you do? Now you're gonna get it." In dog training the words "No" and "Okay" are used for very specific purposes and do their job well. The trick is to use these words *only* to accomplish their designated tasks.

DEFINITION OF "NO"

The word "No" is applied to stop the dog from doing anything that is considered undesirable. It is never accompanied by other words or phrases.

BENEATH THE SURFACE OF THE TRAINING

The most common cause of a dog's confusion is inconsistency in the commands given by his owner. When you want the dog to refrain from jumping on the furniture, stealing food from the table, messing on the floor, or any other bad habit, use only one corrective word: "No." Too often an owner will use ten different corrective words in the course of one day. Words such as "Stop! Don't! Please! Bad dog! Shame!" only communicate anger.

"No" is the most authoritative and negative sound in the language. It is almost impossible to say this word in a positive way. The most timid personality can get the idea across to the animal with "No." If used consistently, the dog will always associate "No" with a bad thing and stop what he's doing instantly. The objective is to create an instant response in the animal to the word "No."

It is important that the word "No" never be associated with the dog's name. If it is he will associate his name with a bad thing. The consequences are great. For instance, in all action commands the dog's name is used before giving the actual command, i.e., *"Silver,* heel"; "Pete, come." But if the dog associates his name with a bad thing, he will never come to you on command or do anything associated with his name except slink away in fear. With a little practice you will discover that "No" used as a correction without any other word will do the job perfectly.

One other point is necessary with this correction. Do not use the word "No" more than once with each correction. Correct the dog with precision rather than a display of emotion. Most dogs respond badly to hyperemotionalism and pick it up as part of their own behavior. If you shout "No, no, no" in a shrill voice you might create a nervous, high-strung, and very neurotic animal. The way to make the correction is with a firm, authoritative vocal sound that comes from the diaphragm. This is accomplished by taking in a deep breath and allowing the stomach to expand with air. Say the word "No" as you release the air. With practice, your tone will resonate and become deeper. One deep-sounding "No" will get the job done, free from emotional damage to the dog. Your voice should indicate a no-nonsense attitude rather than an angry shout, or worse. The point of the command is to get his attention and mildly startle him. Don't make him collapse with fear and urinate uncontrollably in the wake of thundering wrath. "No" simply gets his attention and indicates to him that he is doing something wrong.

The reverse of this problem is using the correction in too mild a manner. Do not take on the tone and style of a doting grandmother with whining, nagging phrases like, "Ohhh, what did you do now, Wolfgang?" Well, sly little Wolfgang knows he has a sucker and can get away with just about anything. It is quite common for an owner to avoid authority in his corrections for fear of losing the animal's love and attention. The truth of the matter is that the animal is grateful to know, once and for all, what he can and cannot do. His respect and love grow in leaps and bounds when he knows *exactly* how to please his master. The dog wants to get along and be accepted with love and affection. If given praise for what he does properly and authoritative corrections when he is behaving badly, he will consistently work for the praise. Dogs, like children, have a keen appreciation for consistency and justice.

PROCEDURE AND TECHNIQUE FOR "NO"

With a firm, authoritative voice give the command "No" for any situation where you want the dog to stop what he is doing. Never use his name. Give him time to respond to the command. Some dogs obey immediately, while others take a second or two before complying. Depending on the breed and temperament of the individual dog, it will take between one and five seconds. One "No" is all you should say. Once the dog has obeyed, praise him for it. This is the beginning of making him work for praise. It is not the word itself that gets the results. It's the *way* you say it. The sound must come from deep within the stomach and indicate a cool authority rather than an emotional anger. You should not have to repeat the correction, otherwise something is wrong. Try using more firmness in your voice. Under no circumstances hit the dog. The word "No" is a key factor in correcting the dog during all training sessions.

The correction "No" is also used with a "throw can" in conjunction with housebreaking and paper training. The "throw can" is explained in detail in Chapter 2. When the dog misbehaves and doesn't respond to "No" as well as he should, shake the can behind your back and then deliver the vocal correction. Dog training is the rare exception where "No" accentuates the positive.

DEFINITION OF "OKAY"

This word is used in several ways. It is used when calling your dog as an affirmative prefix to his name. "Okay" is also a release from training sessions and a release from walking by your side when he has to use the street to relieve himself.

BENEATH THE SURFACE
OF THE TRAINING

"Okay" is a positive command. It should represent a pleasant experience for the dog. The word is essentially a release from discipline. But it is more than that. It is an important word when calling the dog to you. When the dog is far away you must raise your voice to be heard. It could sound like a reprimand and would tend to make the dog hesitate. It implies, "You'd better get here or else." But when you prefix the command with a cheerful "*Okay,* Pete, come," it automatically assures the dog of a happy reception. It is almost impossible to say "Okay" negatively. It seems to make its own cheerful sound because it forces the tone of voice to go higher. Since all the dog wants is love and affection, the use of "Okay" will indicate that everything is fine.

PROCEDURE AND TECHNIQUE
FOR "OKAY"

If one uses the word "Okay," then everything *should* be okay. Do not use the word in any negative context or you will render it useless as a training tool. The word is still considered a command even though it is a light, breezy one. It should make the dog aware that something pleasant is going to happen.

As a release. Assuming he is housebroken, a good dog walks by his owner's left side when on his way to the area in which he relieves himself. He is only allowed three feet of the leash while the rest is gathered up in the owner's hand. This prevents him from leaving the owner's side. When they arrive at the designated place, the owner says "Okay" in a pleasant tone of voice and allows the extra length of the leash to slip through his hand. The dog should then be led off the sidewalk and into the street. He will soon begin to understand what is expected of him if he is *consistently* made to walk by his owner's side until he arrives at the designated area. "Okay" will become a very important word for him. If the dog's need is urgent, stand clear. It has happened that an owner was forced to change his trousers after releasing the dog.

"Okay" is also used when a training session is finished. "*Okay,* Pete; that's all" should bring a joyful response, unless the dog is exhausted from his lesson, which is often the case. Even so, "Okay" will be a welcome sound. This should always be true throughout the dog's life.

6 / The Corrective Jerk

The "corrective jerk" has nothing to do with the latest dance step or the neighborhood chiropractor. A dog does not speak any language known to man, but there are two basic things he does respond to: your pleasure and your displeasure. The very first thing he must learn is that there is only one way to perform—your way. Therefore, it is important to learn how to communicate your displeasure when he does not perform correctly. Hollering at him or hitting him may get across the idea that he was bad, but then his mind is in no condition to go to the next step, which is—what he should have been doing. The most effective communication technique is the "corrective jerk." It is *the* primary corrective action in this obedience course and will be used over and over again. Its importance cannot be stressed enough. Once this technique is learned, you will have a valuable teaching and corrective tool for as long as you have a dog.

DEFINITION OF THE "CORRECTIVE JERK"

The six-foot training leash is attached to a choke collar which hangs loosely around the dog's neck. The leash is held in the right hand as the dog sits or stands on the left side of the owner. Both are facing the same direction. Three feet of the leash dangle from the collar, across the owner's knees, while the remaining three feet are gathered in the owner's right hand. The leash is jerked to the right, sideways, away from the owner's right thigh. The word "No" is said in a firm tone of voice when the jerk is executed. The jerk is quickly executed so that the right hand returns to its original position in a fraction of a second. During the execution of the jerk the choke collar tightens around the dog's neck giving him a mild sensation. As the owner's right hand returns to its original position,

the choke collar is automatically released and once again
hangs loosely from the dog's neck.

BENEATH THE SURFACE
OF THE TRAINING

This technique will be disturbing and a bit of a shock to the
dog when done for the first time. Although it does not hurt, it
does startle him. The firm "No" reinforces the jerk and leaves
no doubt that the dog has displeased you. This is how he will
learn right from wrong. Whenever the dog refuses to execute
a command or indulges a bad habit, deliver a corrective jerk.
*However, immediately following each corrective jerk, give
him great praise and tell him how good he is.*

It is better to deliver one firm jerk, executed correctly,
than many jerks that are not quite so hard. In the end, ten or
fifteen niggling tugs will not only irritate and exhaust the
animal, but will also produce very poor obedience. Excessive
use of this technique will make any dog "jerk shy." If the
firm "No" is applied with every corrective jerk, eventually
the word, without the jerk, will suffice. This will be the beginning of a conditioned reflex to which the dog will respond
for the rest of his life.

PROCEDURE AND TECHNIQUE
FOR THE "CORRECTIVE JERK"

The first step is learning to hold the leash properly. The six-
foot training leash is held in the right hand as it connects to
the choke collar. The dog is by your left side. Both owner and
dog should be facing the same direction.

Place the thumb of the right hand into the very top of the
loop and hold the rest of the leash with the entire hand. (See
Fig. 3.) Depending upon your height, only two or three feet of
the leash should be hanging across the front of your knees
from the dog's collar. The remainder of the leash hangs from
the right hand, barely touching the outer right thigh. This
means that you are holding both the loop and approximately
half of the leash with the right hand. This allows for a firm

FIGURE 3.
How to hold the six-foot training leash.

hold and absolute control. If the dog should bolt, your thumb will hold the leash firmly in your hand.

To properly execute the corrective jerk. Start by facing the same direction as the dog. He is by your left side with the leash attached to his choke collar. Hold the leash in your right hand. Both hands are hanging down from your sides. The leash is quickly jerked to the right, sideways, away from the outer portion of the right thigh. This is always accompanied by a sharp "No." The arm moves like a spring, your wrist and forearm only being used, as the right hand returns to its original position immediately after the jerk. (See Fig. 4.) The choke collar will have tightened around the dog's neck for a split second and then returned to its loose position. The action is to jerk and then release. The entire movement should take no longer than one second. (See Fig. 5.) Any longer than that may hurt or injure the animal.

When jerking the dog. It should not be so hard as to force his legs to leave the ground. That would be more like a punishment than a correction. The dog may whine or cry out after the first few corrective jerks. Do not be disturbed by this. The worst you may have done is pinch his neck. More than likely the animal is trying to manipulate you into letting him maintain control over the situation as he might have been doing up till now. Some dogs are criers and will emit a shrill squeal to force you to stop making them do what they don't want to do. This is a ploy and does not indicate that the dog is

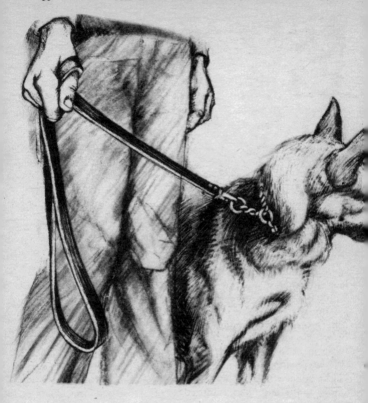

FIGURE 4.
The "corrective jerk."

FIGURE 5.
The "corrective jerk." The right hand holds the leash with several inches of slack. In one quick motion the leash is snapped to the right side and immediately returned to its original position.
All photographs by Mark Handler.

experiencing the slightest bit of pain. Maintain a firm attitude and never let the dog control the situation.

Praise. Immediately following the corrective jerk, give the dog a great deal of enthusiastic praise. Compliments such as "Good boy," "Good dog," "Atta boy," etc., are very effective. Make the praise verbal and do not pet him. A pat on the head very often indicates to a dog that the lesson is over and he can relax. Verbal congratulations are his reward and he needs them in order to know that he has pleased you. This is an aspect of training where many people go wrong. It seems embarrassing to walk down the street talking to your dog. But it is the best thing for a successful training program. Do not be inhibited in expressing affection and enthusiasm for a job well done. Talking to an animal is not as eccentric as it may seem. One talks to an infant even knowing he doesn't understand one word. What one is communicating is approval through emotion. Most humans and domestic animals respond to it. Communicative vocal praise produces greater results than most head pats and body rubs. In this way you are expressing approval without sacrificing disciplinary demands.

When teaching yourself how to execute the corrective jerk, do not practice on the dog. It will exhaust him and create confusion. The correction is merely a tool to be used when

teaching the other commands. It is not an end in itself. It would make a lot more sense to practice on a broom handle or stairway banister until you have learned to execute it correctly. *Do not correct the dog for something he didn't do.* It is counterproductive and unfair. The corrective jerk is a technique—not a person.

7/ "Sit"

Have you ever seen a dog ignore his master when given a command? It is painful to watch the man's face redden and his voice progress from one octave to another as he yells, "Sit. . . . Sit. . . . SIT. . . . *SIT!!!*" Perhaps you've been that man. He has no idea how to communicate with his dog and he doesn't know what to communicate. Commands should be precise and consistent. For that reason each command is defined at the beginning of every chapter. The same command should not be given with a different expectation each time. The command "Sit" is incorrect if used to stop a dog from barking, from running, or from urinating on your friend's leg. None of these have a single thing to do with "Sit."

DEFINITION OF "SIT"

On command, the dog sits erect with all his weight on his haunches. His body is upright and his front legs are straight and slant inward at the top to a slight degree. His mien is proud, his head straight, and his eyes are looking forward.

BENEATH THE SURFACE
OF THE TRAINING

Sitting is a natural position for a dog. But having him sit on command requires patient training and a good understanding of why and when you want him to sit. His inclination to sit occurs when he is curious and wants to observe. The command is one of the best techniques to gain quick control of his behavior when something is overexciting him or distracting him from your purposes. If the doorbell rings, for example, he may start barking or running frantically to the door. In order to control this burst of energy and avoid scaring your caller half to death, undercut the dog's reaction by controlling his behavior. Putting him in the "Sit" would accomplish this if the dog could respond to that command in the middle of his mischief. But he cannot because of his limited mental capacity. He must be made to stop what he's doing first, and then he can be commanded to do something else. Therefore, give him the command "No" first, and "Sit" immediately afterward. If the dog were to get loose while on the street, it would be a life-saving factor to be able to trigger the mechanism in his brain that makes him sit at your command. If trained properly he cannot refuse your command unless he is running at top speed or is involved in an intense dog fight. But even then you will have some control.

From this chapter to the end of the obedience course it is important that you do not feed the dog before beginning training sessions. Otherwise he will be too sluggish to respond properly. Starting with "Sit," every command taught thereafter will require every ounce of concentration the dog possesses. If his stomach is full he will not want to learn. It is also important to allow the dog to relieve himself if the session is conducted outdoors.

PROCEDURE AND TECHNIQUE FOR "SIT"

Whenever teaching this or any other command you must have absolute control and attention. The main tools for exercising this control are the six-foot leash and the choke collar. Nothing can be accomplished without them.

Since this will be the first command the dog will be taught, try to make it as easy as possible for him by giving him the benefit of little or no distraction at all. Take him to a quiet, out-of-the-way place in your neighborhood or to a secluded room indoors. There should be no audience! It will be less inhibiting for both you and the dog. If the lesson is being conducted outdoors, allow the dog to relieve himself before beginning. Otherwise he will not be able to concentrate.

Like most commands, "Sit" requires that you *do not* use the dog's name before giving the command. Only prefix his name to those commands that involve forward motion. The two forward or action commands in this course are "Heel" and "Come."

The leash. Because the leash and the choke collar are of primary importance, their use will once again be described as in Chapter 6. The six-foot training leash is held with the right hand and the dog stays by your left side. Both dog and owner face the same direction. Place the thumb of the right hand into the very top of the loop and hold the rest of the leash with the entire hand. Only two or three feet of the leash should be hanging across the front of your knees from the dog's collar to your right hand. It is easier to maintain control with a shorter length of leash.

Giving the command. Once positioned correctly with the leash properly placed in your hand, give the command "Sit." With your *left hand* push on his haunches until he is in a sitting position. If this is done too hard or too fast it will startle him and he will jump up and move around. Give the command with gentle authority and push on his haunches slowly. When he reaches the proper position praise him. (See Fig. 6.) "Good boy. That's a good dog. Attaboy." Try not to use your hands when giving praise. If he's a puppy he may nip. An older dog may take an affectionate stroke or pat on the head as a sign that the lesson is over. Develop a tone of voice that suggests praise and satisfaction with the dog's performance.

From this point on it is simply a matter of repetition. Repeat the process until he begins to sit without the use of your left hand. It will not take very long. This is the teaching process. It is very important that no correction be given during the teaching process. It is pointless to correct him in something he has not yet learned.

Once he has learned to respond to "Sit" and he fails to do so, the corrective jerk is then used. In this first session repeat the teaching process ten or fifteen times and give him a rest. Do not give him a reason to believe it is now playtime. Just stop and walk around a little, but do not release him from the session. After the break, go back to the command and repeat it again another ten or fifteen times. Both halves of the session should not last more tnan fifteen or twenty minutes. It is quite possible that he will have learned the command in the first session. If not, give him another session, but wait at least one hour. You may give two sessions a day.

FIGURE 6.
*The teaching technique for the command
"Sit." The left hand pushes the
dog into proper position as the
command "Sit" is given.*

Using the corrective jerk. If the dog is still having problems learning the command after several sessions, employ the corrective jerk. With the dog close to your side, take up all but two or three feet of the leash. Give the command "Sit," and gently pull or jerk up on the leash with your right hand and push his haunches down with your left. Once he is in the sitting position give him his praise. This is vital. Repeat the command; pull him with the right hand; lower him with the left. As he sits, give him his praise. Repeat this process until he sits immediately after your command. Do not give him time to consider the command once it is given and never say the command more than once without forcing him to respond properly.

This leads us to the basic training formula of this course: command, correction, and praise. It applies to the teaching of every command. Assuming the dog has been taught the command and he knows it, apply the corrective jerk whenever he does not respond properly. If he ignores you or simply doesn't obey when you say "Sit," snap the leash to the right and sharply say "No!" He will sit because he has been reminded to do so. Remember the formula: command, correction, and praise. If he responds to your command then go right to the praise. If not, execute a corrective jerk and *then* give him his praise. The secret of successful dog training is immediate praise after every correction or command. The dog knows he has pleased you and begins to work for your approval. Verbal praise will spare you the discomfort of fifteen years of bribery.

8 / The "Heel" and "Automatic Sit"

If a human being is referred to as a "heel" it is accepted that he is a bounder, a rotter, one who will take advantage of attractive females and doublecross his friends. If he is "well heeled" he is equipped with much money. But a well-heeled dog is quite another matter. This refers to a dog who *walks in heel,* which is to say, a dog that does not pull his master down the street like an Alaskan sled. The bounding energy of a dog out for his first walk offers little pleasure unless he is trained to "Heel," especially if he is the size of a small horse.

DEFINITION OF "HEEL"

Heeling is having the dog walk on your left side with his head next to your thigh. He walks when you walk and stops when you do. When executed properly, the dog never leaves your side. (See Fig. 7.)

BENEATH THE SURFACE
OF THE TRAINING

Don't throw this book across the room and say, "I'll never get Killheart to do that for me." Although it sounds like a great deal to accomplish, it's not as hard as it seems. The alternatives are unpleasant. If the dog does not "Heel" properly you will either be yanked down the street like a Brahman bull rider at the Rodeo or you will be dragging him along the sidewalk with fifteen meddling "animal lovers" giving you enough guilt to wear away the lining of your stomach. Heeling is not a trick and is not too difficult to teach. Because it does not conform with the natural instincts of the dog, he must be taught to do this with patience, diligence, and repetition.

Everything out of doors is new and exciting, especially to a young puppy, and the street holds a thousand adventures in sight and smell. His natural inclinations are toward curiosity and the indulgence of animal impulses. As in every lesson, do not feed your dog before beginning a training session. Otherwise he will be too sluggish to respond properly.

If the session is conducted outdoors, allow the dog to relieve himself. Otherwise he's in no condition to learn something new. Find a quiet outdoor area with a minimum of distraction. The dog's first response to the outside will be to run ahead, straining at the leash as he pulls you down the street. In his excitement he becomes an absolute ingrate and forgets all you've done for him. Thus it becomes important to teach him that you are the most important factor when out for a walk or a training session.

The dog's spirit is going to be high as he is walked to the training place. Not wanting him to dread each session, try not to discourage his pleasant, happy feeling.

In order to succeed in training your dog you must learn to communicate. This implies that there is a kind of language to be developed. Dogs are like babies that never grow up. An infant responds to the tone, volume, and pitch of the voice speaking to it. Dogs respond in much the same way. The word "No" delivered in a firm tone will stop most dogs in their tracks.

Gaining the dog's attention without a correction is accomplished by pitching the voice high and speaking as you would to a baby. "That's a *good* boy!" Affection and praise are given softly and sincerely. If the dog is trained to sit on command, he will do it properly if you say "liver." It is all in the voice.

PROCEDURE AND TECHNIQUE FOR THE "HEEL"

Limit each session to fifteen minutes and conduct no more than two sessions a day, spaced at least one hour apart.

Proper position. The first step in teaching the "Heel" is putting your dog in the proper position. Place him in the "Sit" position on your left side. Choosing the left side is merely

FIGURE 7.
"Heel" and "Automatic Sit." After the command "Heel" is given, start out with your left foot. Allow several inches of slack in the leash. The dog's head is even with your left thigh. When you stop, the dog does as well and goes into the "Sit" position.

traditional. It began as a safety factor for hunters who carried their weapons with their right arm while the dog walked astride on the left.

Using the six-foot leash, hold it in your right hand as if you were going to execute the corrective jerk. Both arms should hang loose and unbent. Always allow two or three feet of slackened leash to drape across the knees. Do not hold the leash with two hands. That would merely be holding on to the animal. Do not let the right hand rise to your chest. You cannot jerk properly unless the right hand is by your side.

Using his name. Once you and the dog are in the correct position and ready to go, give the command, "Pete, heel!" Use his name this time because "Heel" is an action command and it alerts him to move into a forward position. Saying his name first gets his attention. Once his name is said, the dog's focus should be on you. He should be ready to move. At the command, "Pete, heel," start walking by starting with your left foot. The reason one starts with the left foot is because it is closer to the dog's eyes and he will move when you do. In this way you will move together. Remember, the objective is to have the dog walk at your side.

If the dog runs ahead. The first problem you will probably encounter is the dog's desire to run ahead. The best way to solve this is to allow him to run to the end of the six-foot training leash. As he reaches the end of it make a quick right turn. At the moment of impact give a loud, authoritative "Heel." Immediately walk in the opposite direction. The dog will have been jolted and forcibly turned in the direction you are walking. (See Fig. 8.) Once again his primitive instincts will have been totally thwarted by your will.

Certain breeds will cry out in shock louder than others. Do not express the slightest concern or sympathy. Keep walking at a brisk clip and the dog will catch up. When he does, adjust the leash to the length with which you started. If the dog shoots ahead of you again, repeat the procedure. Make a quick right turn, say "Heel," and walk in the opposite direction. This business of turning in the opposite direction is hard on the dog. Therefore he must be praised as he catches up. The praise will help teach him what walking in "Heel" means. It tells him he is good if he walks by your side. It also keeps his attention on you, which prepares him for any stops or turns. *The technique for praising the dog varies from breed to*

FIGURE 8.
*If the dog runs ahead after
being commanded to "Heel,"
make a sharp turn in the
opposite direction and continue walking.*

breed. Either give immediate praise after the sudden turn or withhold it for a few seconds, depending upon the breed of the dog. Some breeds need immediate approval, while others take it to mean they are released from the lesson. Check Part III and find the page pertaining to your breed for this specific information.

Lagging behind. The dog's tendency to run ahead will diminish with each fifteen-minute lesson. Once he is no longer running ahead, be prepared to cope with the problem of lagging behind. This problem is easily solved by extending verbal encouragement if the dog fails to keep up with you. Tell him what a good dog he is, and literally entice him to catch up. A lavish invitation to walk by your side will keep his attention fixed on you and will probably solve the problem. What is desirable is to help the dog develop the habit of keeping his attention on you whenever he is taken for a walk.

Walking by your side. After three or four lessons it will be time to teach the dog his exact position when walking with you. Up to this point he will have been keeping one or two lengths ahead, which is all right. But now he must learn to always walk with his head lined up to your left thigh, no far ther ahead or behind.

As before, start with the dog in the "Sit" position. Give him the command, "Pete, heel." Start walking with your left foot. Every single time the dog's head moves beyond your thigh execute a corrective jerk, sharply say "No," make an immediate right turn, say, "Pete, heel," and continue to walk in the opposite direction. Praise him. This procedure should be repeated again and again until the dog is walking in the prescribed position. It is possible for the dog to learn this in a single fifteen-minute session. However, keep repeating the technique for as long as it takes him to learn it. Do not work the dog for more than fifteen minutes at a time and give him an hour's rest between lessons. Only two lessons a day are permissible.

Too shy to walk. Occasionally a dog is either too shy or too frightened to walk at all on his first encounter with the outside. This is usually associated with puppies. He will cower with fear and probably duck under your legs or look for the protection of the nearest wall. The objective is to rid the dog of his fear. Too much authority will only tend to reinforce his terror and uncertainty. First, try to start him out on the "Heel" command. If he will not walk, step in front of him and go down on your knees. Gently call him with affectionate entreaties and playful calls. Get him to come. Do this about three or four times until he comes every time that you bend down. Once he is doing that start backing away as he comes. Keep lengthening the distance he has to go. Once he is on his feet and walking, stand up, turn, and walk together. If he is a particularly stubborn dog and freezes at this point, keep walking, pulling him along until he gives in. Be careful not to scrape his paw pads too hard along the sidewalk or other hard surfaces. The pads are sensitive and will bleed easily. This could create a trauma which will make the problem acute. If the struggle continues, take him to a park. If the dog again freezes, keep walking as you pull him along the grass. This will prevent a traumatic injury and force the dog to walk with you.

Jumping. If your dog is overexuberant and continually jumps on people on the street during his training session, employ the corrective jerk at the moment of his infraction and sharply say "No." It is important to note that if the dog is corrected for jumping on people, then it must be consistently enforced both indoors and outdoors.

Walking out of "Heel." If the dog is overly affectionate he is probably wrapping himself around your legs. Obviously, this creates an absurd situation. It could be insecurity or acute sensitivity. This is the only instance where one uses the left hand while walking in "Heel." Place the dog in the proper position as you walk, all the while giving him encouragement. His head must always be lined up with your left thigh. If he continues to wrap around your legs, walk and hold him in place with the left hand, utilizing the corrective jerk less frequently than usual and manipulating him more with a soothing tone of voice.

In the beginning it is more important to stress the proper position than the other aspects of heeling. Never use excessive authority to a nervous or frightened dog. Affection and gentleness are the only techniques that will rid him of his fear.

Walking inward. Another problem is when the dog begins to turn inward while heeling, causing both owner and dog to step into each other's paths. This is usually poor navigation on the dog's part and nothing more serious than that. The corrective jerk is the only way to solve this problem. As soon as the dog walks into your path, execute a corrective jerk. At the same time sharply say "No." Then make a left or right turn, depending on how far inward he has gotten. As you turn, your knee will gently force him to turn with you. Praise him. Then say, "Pete, heel." Continue walking. Praise him. Do this every time he gets underfoot.

Whenever the dog becomes distracted, tries to wander off, or turns the session into play, do this: give the corrective jerk. Sharply say "No." Then say, "Pete, heel." Continue to walk. Praise him.

DEFINITION OF THE "AUTOMATIC SIT"

When the dog is walking in "Heel," he must stop when you do and sit without being given a command. He then waits until he is given the next command, which is usually "Heel."

PROCEDURE AND TECHNIQUE FOR THE "AUTOMATIC SIT"

This is accomplished by letting the dog know that you are going to stop. By simply slowing down, he will be alerted to a change of some kind. Because he watches you most of the time, he will slow down, too. As you come to a full stop, give the command "Sit." Do not use the dog's name on this command. *The verbal command is used during the teaching process only.* If the dog fails to sit, use the corrective jerk as a reminder. Do not forget to praise him after he successfully obeys each command, even if he did so after a correction.

If he does not sit. Do not give the command more than once. This should be a firm rule throughout the training. You cannot stand in the street saying "Sit, sit, sit, sit, sit" *ad nauseam* until he finally obeys. Use the corrective jerk and in a sharp voice say "No!" The dog will understand this and sit for you. Praise him for obeying.

To reiterate: slow your pace and gradually come to a full

stop. If the dog does not sit, give the command "Sit." If he does not respond, give him a corrective jerk and a sharp "No!" If he responds properly, praise him with enthusiasm, even though he was corrected. This is his motivation.

In that rare instance when the dog does not respond to the corrective jerk accompanied by the "No," give him a corrective jerk and the command "Sit!" Then slowly pull the leash upward as you force the dog to sit by pushing his haunches down with your left hand. One usually never gives a command with the corrective jerk. It causes the dog to associate a negative emotion with that particular command. However, in this extreme instance it becomes necessary.

How you give the corrective jerk is the key to this problem. One or two hard jerks will save much time and frustration for both you and the dog. He must know that you mean what you say. It will be useful to remember that the word "Sit" is a command and the word "No" is a correction. The commands are given with firmness. The corrections are given with an authoritative tone of voice.

Because every training session should end on a high note, the lesson ought to be terminated when the dog has completed his task successfully for the first time. Obviously, he is not going to be perfect in his execution of your commands for several weeks. Therefore the instant he performs his new command correctly, end the lesson and extend lavish praise. This will help him to remember what he has just learned and to look forward to performing properly the next time. Try to instill in him the idea that training is fun.

9/ "Sit-Stay"

Now that you have taught your dog to "Sit" and to automatically "Sit" after walking in "Heel," the next command is perfectly logical. You want him to "Stay" in his sitting position. It's not as simple as it sounds. Dogs take you at your word, quite literally. If given the command "Sit," a trained dog will sit—for an instant and then move on to whatever interests him. His obligation has been fulfilled, from his point of view. If expected to remain in a sitting position for any length of time, he must be commanded to do so.

DEFINITION OF "SIT-STAY"

Once again, on command, the dog sits erect with all his weight on his haunches. He remains in this position until released from the command . . . no matter what!

BENEATH THE SURFACE OF THE TRAINING

This command is used when you do not want the dog to move. When leaving your home, if the dog follows you to the door, you know he'll dash out the minute it is open. Give the command "Sit" and he'll obey. But as soon as you start to leave he'll be out of the house too. Therefore, give the next command, "Stay."

This command goes against every instinctual impulse the animal has. Most dogs, especially puppies, will follow you to the edge of the world and jump off if you do. The dog wants to go where you go, do what you do, as the song says, then he'll be happy. The pattern is set in the first months of ownership. The dog grows up following you wherever you go, underfoot, in the kitchen, on the couch, and in the bed. By now he is so used to being with you he looks up at you as if you were a lunatic when first given the command "Stay." He will completely disregard the command and race you to wherever you're going.

After the dog has been taught the command "Stay," there will still be times when it will be almost impossible for him to obey. For instance, if there is a party going on in your house he will have a nervous breakdown trying to comply with your command and ignore his impulse to join the fun. Either remove him from the scene or invite him in to be admired and ogled. The same applies if you're cooking a steak in front of his nose. Also, don't expect him to remain in a "Stay" position for eternity. If he will remain in position between fifteen and thirty minutes then he is extraordinary and has been well trained.

The command "Sit-Stay" is not designed for off-leash discipline in the city. If such a foolish thing is attempted, one might well be considered an executioner. The dog in the city may obey perfectly outside for six months, off-leash. But it only takes one infraction of the command for him to chase another dog or pigeon and lose his life to an oncoming automobile.

"Sit-Stay" should be taught indoors with the six-foot leash. Learning the command on the six-foot leash is so vital that there must be no distraction at all. Do not go outdoors for this command until you reach that section of this chapter that calls for working with the twenty-five-foot line.

PROCEDURE AND TECHNIQUE FOR "SIT-STAY"

Teaching this command involves three elements: a voice command, a hand signal, and a pivoting technique on the ball of your left foot.

The voice command and hand signal. Place the dog in the "Sit" position on your left side. Allow him thirty seconds to settle down and get comfortable. Both dog and owner should be facing the same direction. Give the command "Stay" in a firm voice. Because this is not an action command, do not

FIGURE 9.
"Sit-Stay." Start out facing in
the same direction as the dog.
Give the verbal command accompanied by the correct hand
signal. The dog should remain
in position when you move
directly in front of him and
when you move back.

prefix the command with the dog's name. The leash is held in the right hand. Upon giving the command flatten your left hand with all fingers closed together (as for a salute) and place it in front of the dog's eyes four inches away. Do not touch his eyes. Simply block his vision. (See Fig. 9.) The hand signal is given simultaneously with the voice command. As the right hand holds the leash, the left hand extends in front of you four inches and then moves leftward to block the dog's vision. The hand signal is a deliberate but quick gesture. Therefore, you return your left hand to your side two or three seconds after having blocked the dog's vision. Eventually, the dog will respond to this hand signal without the vocal command.

A pivoting technique for the ball of your left foot. You and the dog are facing in the same direction. The objective now is to make one deliberate turn without moving the dog so that you will be facing him. Do not step off with your left foot as you normally would in the "Heel." Step off with your right foot and turn toward the dog. The left foot is used as a pivot and revolves in place. It is all right if the left foot must move a very short distance. Once your body is turned and facing the dog, bring the left foot back to where the right foot has landed so that both feet are together. (See Fig. 10.) If you move your left foot before facing the dog, he is going to assume it's time to "Heel" and start walking.

The secret of teaching him to "Stay." As you pivot in front of him, hold eighteen inches of the leash straight up so that the leash and collar are high on his neck. The remainder of the leash dangles in a slackened loop from the bottom of your right hand. In this position the dog cannot move as you turn to face him. What you are doing is holding him in a fixed position with the extended leash. If the leash is held properly there will be eighteen inches of taut leash extended upward. Do not hold the leash too tightly or he may choke or become frightened and struggle to run.

It is this strict leash control during the pivotal turn that communicates the idea "Stay." The entire movement should be accomplished with dispatch so that he does not have time to think about turning or walking. Keep him in position and get in front of him without wasting a motion. It is going to take ten or fifteen tries before he gets the idea. Do not forget to give the dog praise once you have made the turn and he has remained in position, even though he had to be held there with the leash. (Do not use his name when giving the praise. He will try to move if you do.) Once you are in front of the dog, remain still for ten or fifteen seconds, leash still held high, so that he begins to absorb what's expected of him. This technique of stepping in front of the dog is only used in training. If you are training a puppy do not be too strict.

Backing away as the dog remains in "Stay." Once the dog accepts the leash control as you stand in front of him, it is then time to back away as he remains in "Stay." While still holding the leash above the dog's head, transfer it to the left hand, placing the thumb inside the loop at the very top. With the right hand, grasp the leash eighteen inches above the collar and hold it loosely. The leash must be able to slide through the right hand once you start to move away from the dog. (See Fig. 11.) The technique will eliminate any slack from developing as you move away. This is important. If the leash slackens you will be unable to force the dog to remain in "Sit-Stay."

Using the right hand as a guide for the leash to slide through, begin to back away slowly. If the dog starts to move forward,

FIGURE 10.
Simultaneously giving command and hand signal, pivot on the ball of the left foot.

and he will, give the command "Stay." As you do, step in toward the dog, pull the leash through the right hand and hold it eighteen inches over the dog's head. Keep the leash tight so that it forces the dog to "Sit." (When stepping in, try to pull the leash slightly to the side as you extend it upward. This will avoid hitting the dog on the chin with the metal clip.) The correction will stop the dog from moving. As he repositions himself give him praise for stopping. Wait a few seconds and then continue to back away. Slowly continue to slide the leash through your right hand as you move. You will probably be able to go a little farther back this time before he begins to move again. The instant the dog moves forward repeat the procedure: Give the command "Stay." Step in toward the dog and hold the leash tightly over his head. Praise him for stopping after he repositions himself. Continue to back away until you reach the end of the six feet of leash. Reinforce this instruction by repeating the entire process ten times.

Walking around either side of the dog as he remains in "Stay." It is now time to condition the dog so that you can walk around him or to either side without his violating the "Stay" command. Usually when you walk to the dog's side or behind him while he is in "Stay," he will turn his head to watch and then turn his entire body to face you. This is a violation of the command. If he is allowed to move that much then it will soon become permissible to move away completely. He must remain in the same position in which he was originally placed. A certain amount of head turning is inevitable, but that is all.

Once again, standing in front of the dog, hold the leash tightly eighteen inches above his head with your right hand. Take one or two steps to the right without loosening up on the leash and then return. Do the same thing again but move to the left. This will condition the dog to your side movements while he is still held in place. Repeat this ten times. Return to the original "Sit" position with the dog at your left side and repeat the entire lesson to this point five times.

Walking behind the dog as he remains in "Stay." Once again hold the leash with your left hand. Standing in front of the dog, slide your right hand in on the leash and extend it over the dog's head about eighteen inches. As you hold the dog in place, begin a brisk but deliberate circular walk around the dog. If he starts to move tighten up on the leash and repeat the command "Stay." When walking around the dog take large steps. The command should be given in a low, soothing voice that reassures. However, it is the subtle use of the leash that is your line of communication.

The leash is comparable to the reins of a horse. Although it is extended upward, it does not tighten unless the dog tries to move. The moment he stops moving you loosen up a bit. A horse respects a rider the minute he mounts him if the rider knows how to handle the reins. The same applies to a dog. If an owner is in control, with the use of the leash and collar, the dog will respect him and submit to his authority.

The minute he observes a lack of consistent control he is going to disobey. In turn the owner will get frustrated and angry and the lesson will be shot.

Because "Stay" is difficult for your dog to learn, do not attempt to teach everything in one training session. Give him a chance to learn it slowly. Sometimes it takes several sessions for the dog to get accustomed to your pivot. When teaching more than one phase of this command in one day rest one hour between each phase. Do not teach more than two sessions a day. Dogs tire and bore easily and after a point lose their ability to pay attention. It is more important that

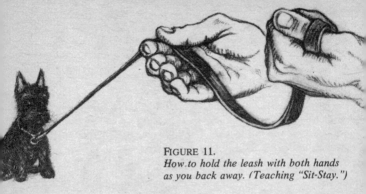

FIGURE 11.
*How to hold the leash with both hands
as you back away. (Teaching "Sit-Stay.")*

the dog learn well and obey when given a command than learn
quickly and forget the command two days later.

"SIT-STAY," OFF-LEASH, OUTDOORS

Now that you and the dog have learned the basic "Stay"
command we come to the very difficult aspect of that command, and that is "Stay" while off the leash. Taking the dog
off the leash is a very dangerous practice and there are few
occasions when it is justified. But assuming you are in a safe,
no-traffic locale or a fenced-in area, it can be taught with
patience and diligence. Off-leash training is optional.

A twenty-five-foot clothesline. In order to teach the "Stay"
off-leash, you will need a twenty-five-foot training leash or
clothesline. However, before going into this lesson make
certain that the dog is thoroughly trained to sit in the "Stay"
position with the six-foot leash attached to his collar. If he
cannot accomplish that then teaching him the "Stay" off-
leash will be a waste of time. The point of the long leash or
clothesline is to keep extending the distance between you
and the dog while he is placed in "Stay." He may "Stay" at
six feet, but will he "Stay" at twelve feet? It is desirable for
him to respond off the leash, but he will never accomplish
that if he is not *perfect* while on the leash. There is no shortcut
or substitute for accomplishing this command.

The same technique. In teaching "Stay" off the leash, you use the same technique outlined in teaching the "Stay" while on-leash with one difference. You keep extending the length of the leash two feet each time the dog holds the position properly. Starting with eight feet of leash proceed by walking around the dog after placing him in "Stay." Each time he holds still extend the leash another two feet. At the dog's back, during your circular walk around him, take up some of the leash by sliding it through your right hand so that you will be much closer to him. In that manner a correction can be given if he moves. When coming around the other side let out the leash to the length you started with. If the dog moves during any part of this procedure execute a corrective jerk and a sharp "No." It is good form to correct the animal now that he has learned the basics of the command.

Extend the clothesline two feet at a time. Do not go from eight feet to twenty feet in one or two lessons. It is important to go methodically in two-feet increments. He must learn to "Stay" at six feet, eight feet, ten feet, twelve feet, and soon to the end of the line or it will be a waste of time. At eighteen or twenty feet it will be difficult to deliver an effective corrective jerk. However, by accompanying the corrective jerk with the sharp "No" at the shorter distances, the "No" itself will almost suffice at the longer distances. That is, providing your "No" has always been very firm. By this time he is associating your "No" with the corrective jerk and will understand on a vocal level alone. Once he starts responding to your "No" while on the leash, it will have the same effect with the leash removed. This conditions the dog psychologically to associate the firm "No" with the hard corrective jerk. Eventually he will stop whatever he's doing when corrected vocally.

At the end of his rope. Once twenty or twenty-five feet of line have been reached it is not unusual for the dog to break and run the other way, even though he has been placed in "Stay." He may see another dog or go butterfly chasing. In this event let him reach the end of the line and then jerk him in the opposite direction with full force and yell "No" as loudly and as harshly as you can. This is the ultimate correction and will be long remembered by your dog.

You are now ready to try him off the leash. Do not attempt this unless absolutely certain he will remain in "Stay" for the full length of the twenty-five-foot leash. When ready for the big moment be certain you remove the leash in a closed-in area. If he breaks or moves once having been placed in "Stay," deliver a very firm "No." If he does not respond properly *do not punish him.* Simply go back to the twenty-five-foot line and work him some more. Eventually he will respond properly.

Another aspect of "Stay" has to do with placing him in that position and leaving the room. It can be useful and convenient from time to time. Place the dog in the "Sit" position. Hook the six-foot leash to his collar and let it drop to the floor. Start out by placing him in "Stay" and leaving the room. Do not forget to use the hand signal. Return in five seconds. If he did not move, praise him. Do this ten times. The next step is to leave the room for ten seconds, return, and praise him for his good performance. It is assuring him that you are not really leaving. Gradually increase the length of time out of the room until he will "Stay" by himself for at least five minutes. Once again, do not do this off the leash until it is certain that he will "Stay" without moving. The leash, even though it is not being held, represents the line of authority between you and the dog. He knows and respects it. A good way to practice this command is to put it in operation right away during everyday household situations. If he approaches the garbage can when the lid is off, put him in "Sit-Stay" until it is covered. The same applies when the doorbell rings or a visitor enters the house. This kind of practice plus his regular lessons will help round off his schooling perfectly.

Once the dog has completely learned the meaning of the command "Stay," you can, with confidence, leave him in a room alone, or talk with friends or tradesmen as he sits still. This command will also keep him out of intimate situations that do not concern him. Every dog is a born voyeur and the command "Stay" could save your marriage. Work hard on this one!

10/ "Down" and "Down-Stay"

Professional dog trainers often are confronted with seemingly difficult problems that are easily solved. One recent client is a musician who owns a magnificent Basset Hound. He named his dog "Cat." In the parlance of contemporary musicians this designation is a compliment. (The name gathers no blue ribbons in Dogdom, however.) It seems that Cat had a problem. He couldn't sit like a dog. Owing to his long, heavy body and his short legs it was impossible for him to "Sit-Stay" for more than a few seconds. His "Sit" was sloped at a ten-degree angle. He looked like a jacked-up car with a flat tire. Too much weight rested on those short front legs and Cat had to get off his "dogs" quickly. It was then that the "Down" and "Down-Stay" was taught.

Even though you may not own a Basset Hound, your dog may have Cat's problem to some degree. The "Sit-Stay" position is a temporary one and is used for short periods of time. But if the dog is to stay in his corner while guests are being entertained, employ the "Down" and "Down-Stay." It's more comfortable for the dog and dictates a longer staying time to him. It was a great relief for Cat and will be for your dog, too. Does all this seem confusing? Well, think of poor Cat, the dog!

DEFINITION OF "DOWN"

The dog is on the ground, head erect, eyes looking forward. The front legs are extended and the hind legs relaxed with the rear weight resting on both haunches. The hind legs should be equally tucked under in a straight parallel.

BENEATH THE SURFACE
OF THE TRAINING

The "Down" position is probably the most comfortable one for the dog. But it may take the longest period of time to teach. Sitting and walking are natural movements for a dog and are assimilated as commands quite easily. But going down on command is unnatural for him, even though he sleeps and rests in that position. Quite often the command "Down" is given as a remedy for undesirable behavior. "Down" should be used only as a command. As outlined in the "Sit-Stay" chapter, you cannot go directly into a command when the dog is misbehaving until a correction has been made first.

In the "Procedure and Technique for Down,' " which follows, you will see that a hand signal is used to help the dog perform properly. The hand signal entails using your unbent, extended arm in a slow downward sweep with the flattened palm of the hand facing the ground. This hand signal may be problematic if the dog has been hit. When he sees that hand come down, his first reaction will be fear. Naturally, he will think he is about to be hit again. The dog probably will have the same reaction when someone reaches out to pet him. He will either run away, flinch, or literally bite the hand that feeds him. This condition is called "hand shy."

If your dog is hand shy you must cease hitting him. It is now time to convince him that hands reaching out to him or commanding him mean something good rather than the smack on the snout they too often represented in the past. If the dog has been hit over a long period of time, or has been hit severely, then it is too late. He will never be able to be taught this command with a hand signal. You will have to rely on the voice command only. You may try extending your hand while lavishing him with praise and affection. If applied long enough this may possibly recondition the dog's reaction. However, if it's not too late, refrain from ever using your hand for anything other than hand signals or affectionate praise or love. This rule also precludes the use of the hand for threats, violent gestures, or even disciplinary pointing. Pointing your finger at the dog and saying "Naughty, naughty" produces the same negative effect.

There are many occasions when the "Down" and "Down-Stay" are useful and make life more comfortable. When you're having company for dinner it is extremely difficult for Gusman to keep his nose out of things. In the "Down" and "Down-Stay" position he is able to participate in the festivities without getting into trouble. These commands are extremely useful outdoors, if, for example, you want to sit on a park bench without being disturbed by a dog pulling on his leash. The main reason this position works so well is because it is comfortable and relaxing for the dog.

Because of the difficulty involved in teaching this command, it is important to be alone with the animal. Do not expect him to learn it in one lesson. Take as long as is necessary. Maintain only two sessions a day, spaced at least one hour apart. Each session must be confined to fifteen minutes. Before starting each session work the dog in his other commands in order to get him in the proper frame of mind. Only teach as much in one day as the dog can absorb. It is interesting to note that the dog will learn "Down" and "Down-Stay" better than any other command he has been taught. The reason is that more time and diligence are required in the teaching than any other aspect of this course. You will also be using these commands more often than any other during the course of a single day. These sessions will prove to be the most rewarding. There is nothing more gratifying than raising your hand in the air when the dog is five or ten feet away and watching him go down as you lower your hand.

PROCEDURE AND TECHNIQUE FOR "DOWN"

Putting the dog down as you stand by his side. Always place the dog in a "Sit-Stay" position to begin each session. Stand by his right side as in the "Heel," holding the leash in whichever hand is most comfortable. Both you and the dog face the same direction. Kneel down on your left knee. In a firm voice give the command "Down," and with your free hand pull his two front paws forward so that he has no choice but to ease himself to the ground. Place your index finger between his two paws so that you can grip both of them with one hand. (See Fig. 12.) The reason for separating his paws with your finger is so they do not get crushed together.

To recap: you and the dog are facing the same direction as in the "Heel." The dog is in the "Sit-Stay" position. The

FIGURE 12.
"Down" and "Down-Stay."
When pulling the dog's paws
forward to teach him "Down"
be sure to separate them
with your index finger. This
avoids pain for the dog.

leash is held in the right hand. Give the command "Down," and as you kneel reach in front of the dog, take his two front paws in your hand (separating them with your index finger), and pull them forward, forcing him down.

For the command "Down" the vocal intonation is different from all others. The very word must be said in an exaggerated manner so that the sound suggests to the dog a downward motion. The tone of your voice should descend in pitch as the dog obeys the command and goes down. Stretch out the middle part of the word so that you do not finish saying it until the dog has reached the ground. This is done by elongating the "ow" part of "D-o-w-n." Somewhere in the middle of the elongated "ow" the voice should descend so that it accompanies the downward action of the dog. It looks like this on paper: "DOWWWWWwwn." Dogs do not understand words as well as they understand intonations. "DOWWWWW-wwwn" is a sound they remember all their lives.

Maintain control with the use of the leash. If the dog gets up in the middle of the session use the leash to place him in the "Sit-Stay" position again. Do not give him a corrective jerk or any other kind of correction. That is never done when teaching a new command. Actually, the leash is used primarily to keep the dog in a sitting position as you slowly give the command and pull his paws forward.

Each time the dog goes down give him praise and congratulations. At this stage, however, he may roll on his side. Give him praise, anyway. It is for going down on command (even though he was pulled). The important thing at this stage is that he learn the most fundamental meaning of the command "Down." He may play or get frisky once he is on the ground. Let him. That can always be corrected later. This procedure should be repeated ten or fifteen times until he offers no resistance when his paws are pulled forward. If you're very lucky he may begin to go down without your hands pulling him.

Putting the dog down as you stand in front of him. The object here is to get the dog to go down while you stand in front of him, face to face. This is important if he is to obey the command when he stands a good distance away from you.

Again, put the dog in the "Sit-Stay" position. Move in front of him and proceed as before. Kneeling on one foot, give the command "DOWWWWWwwwn," and pull his front paws forward with your right hand. The position of the leash is a little more awkward this time because it will be held above and to the left of the dog's head with your left hand. The leash becomes very important here. Some dogs will have a tendency to walk toward you if you are facing them. The dog must be held in place with the leash without a formal correction. You will probably not have to repeat this step as often as the first one since it is mostly the same movement but in a different position.

Repeat this procedure ten or fifteen times and quit for the day.

The hand signal for "Down" as you stand by his side. You now start introducing the hand signal with the voice command. To do so go back to the side position. Always start out in this position because it makes it easier to control the dog. It offers fewer distractions and allows the hand to manipulate the leash with greater authority. If the dog has ever been hit, or for some inexplicable dog reason doesn't like this command, he may attempt to bite when you use the hand signal. Begin the lesson in the side position because it offers greater safety.

You are now in the "Heel" position, but with one knee on the ground. Hold the leash with your right hand and leave your left hand free. The leash is extended to the right of the dog in front of your body. There should be absolutely no slack in the leash. Allow about twelve inches from his collar to your right hand. If the dog tries to jump up on you in a playful manner simply raise the leash so that he has no room to do anything but sit. Command him to "Sit," give him a "Good boy," and return your right hand to its original position.

Stay in a cheerful mood and do not say anything harsh. This is the crucial part of the lesson. Bring your left hand up above the dog's eye level and slightly to the right of his head. Keep it flattened, fingers closed, palm down. With your right hand make sure that the leash is taut. This is very important. If your left hand is positioned properly it should be in sight of the dog's peripheral vision.

Give the dog the vocal command "DOWWWWWwwwn" as you begin to lower your left hand to the ground. As your hand goes down it will press on the leash where the metal clasp connects with the collar ring. (See Fig. 13.) The dog is pushed to the ground by the force of the hand against the leash. Because the dog sees your flattened hand push him

FIGURE 13.
"Down" and "Down-Stay."
Teaching the dog to go down
by pushing the leash downward with the left hand
while kneeling by the side of
the dog.

down, he will always associate that hand gesture with his cue to go down. It should not take too many repetitions for him to offer little or no resistance. The point is that he has already been taught the meaning of the vocal command "DOWWWWWwwwn" and will know what to do. Of course, it took the first two steps to get to this point. If the dog resists or offers opposition, just keep pushing down and don't worry if the collar tightens up. Once he's down, lavish him with praise. If he really fights hard on this lesson stop immediately, tell him he's a good boy, and go into the "Heel" and the "Sit" and then start over.

Exercise patience and the strictest control over your temper. The dog cannot be intimidated into learning this lesson. He must be brought around to it with persistence and the reassurance that it pleases you. Reposition yourself and place the dog in "Sit-Stay." Hold the leash tautly in your right hand and kneel. Place your flattened left hand on top of the leash near the clip, give the command "DOWWWWWwwwn," and push the tightened leash to the ground. When the dog touches the ground congratulate him with a "Good boy" in a cheerful voice. Let him know that you are very pleased with him. This is very hard work for the dog and it will tire him quickly. Every ounce of concentration he possesses is being utilized. Give him at least an hour's rest after this session.

The hand signal while standing in front of him. You are now going to be standing in front of the dog. He saw the hand from the side force him down. Now he is going to see it from the front. It was important that your hand was first seen from the side. It represented no threat of hitting him. It will now be easier for him to accept the hand signal from the front because he is familiar with it.

From "Heel" place the dog in "Sit-Stay," then step in front of him. Hold the leash, with the left hand, to your left side. This gives you greater control as you push down. Kneel on one knee, raise your right hand, palm down, on top of the leash and push it to the ground. At the same time give the vocal command "DOWWWWWwwwn." Once the dog is on the ground he may try to nip playfully at your fingers. As long as it doesn't hurt it is permissible and can be corrected at a time when he knows the command perfectly. If, however, the dog tends to hide or play between your knees, exercise control with the leash by placing him in "Sit-Stay" and starting all over. Repeat this entire step until the dog is performing with no resistance. This is as far as you should go in one day. End the session on a happy note and continue the next day. Resist the temptation to show the new command to your friends and relatives until it is absolutely certain the dog has thoroughly printed it in his mind.

Without kneeling. Review the training of the preceding sessions. The object of this step is to get the dog to respond to "Down" with a vocal command and a hand signal as you stand in front of him *without kneeling.* Stand in front of the dog and stay about eighteen inches away. Place the dog in the "Sit-Stay" position. Hold the leash with your left hand. If he tries to get up, tighten the leash by raising it above his head. This will hold him in place. Even if the dog doesn't obey the command properly he will be forced to sit and wait for you to correct him or reinstruct him.

For this step leave half the leash slack (three feet of the six-foot training leash). Raise your right arm and flatten your hand, palm down, as if for a salute. Give the vocal command "DOWWWWWwwwn." As you say the command start lowering your arm. Bring the flat of your hand to the top of the slackened leash, which should be held at an angle to your left. (See Fig. 14.) The dog should go down without having to be forced by the leash. Give him an enthusiastic "Good boy" and repeat the step ten times.

From a farther distance. After a short rest repeat the procedure but from a farther distance. You were eighteen inches away before, now extend the distance to three feet. You are still at a distance where the dog can be corrected if he gets too playful or does not respond to the command properly. If he starts to move away or come forward, give him a corrective jerk and a firm "No." It is acceptable to use the corrective jerk now because the dog is quite familiar with the command. You are no longer teaching the basics of the "Down" but rather the refinements.

Once again, raise your arm with a flattened hand as if for a salute. While saying "DOWWWWWwwwn," bring your arm down with the palm facing the ground. Only this time, the hand goes past the leash without touching it. (See Fig. 15.) This is the hand signal as it will always look. Visually it is the lowering of the arm as it returns to its natural position by the side of the body. At this point the dog thinks you are

FIGURE 14.
"Down" and "Down-Stay."
Pushing the leash downward
while standing in front of
the dog.

FIGURE 15.
"Down" and "Down-Stay."
Proper hand signal for
"Down."

FIGURE 16.
Proper hand signal for "Down."

going to touch the top of the leash and force him down. His response will be to go into the "Down" position in anticipation of being pushed down. The movement will soon become natural for him and will never require anything more than a lowering of your raised arm. (See Fig. 16.) Once the dog knows this position, you will be able to execute the command with the hand signal or with the voice command only. Practice giving the command "DOWWWWWwwwn" without the hand signal. Repeat the vocal procedure alone several times and then switch to giving the signal alone. End the session by using both hand signal and voice command. Remember, a great quantity of praise is necessary in this lesson. Lavish the dog with praise every time he performs properly. But never use his name during his praise or he's going to get up and walk toward you.

If the dog acts confused when you give the hand signal without the voice command, repeat the signal several times. If he still does not respond then go back to giving the hand signal accompanied by the voice command. Immediately afterward, try the hand signal alone. This process should reinforce his understanding of what is expected of him. What's important is the consistency between your hand descending and the tone of your voice descending in the elongated command "DOWWWWWwwwn." Once he executes the command to your satisfaction, stop work. End the lesson on a high note.

An alternate method for oversized dogs. The technique outlined in this chapter will always work if applied properly. However, there is one exception. If the dog is oversized it will be awkward or difficult to use the leash in the same manner. Therefore, instead of pushing the leash with your flattened hand, use your foot. By this it is meant that the leash is in the right hand and held in place with the left foot. (See Fig. 17.) The trick is to run the leash under your shoe in the space between the heel and the sole. Sliding the leash through the arch gives leverage to your hand and will force the dog to the ground while you lower your left arm as described before. Give the voice command "DOWWWWWwwwn" and slowly pull up on the leash as you lower your left arm past his eyes. Do not pull up on the leash too quickly or you'll have a fight on your hands. Be careful not to hurt the animal, otherwise this will always be an unhappy command for him. Do it slowly, gently, and firmly. Extend the voice command

FIGURE 17.
*"Down." Method for teaching
"Down" to an oversized dog.
Run the leash under your
shoe in the space between the
heel and the sole.*

to match the time it takes to pull him to the "Down" position. When he is in position give him an expansive, "Good boy!" Once he's down and tries to get up, simply hold the leash with the sole of your shoe so he won't be able to move. Use this technique only if the dog is too large to push down with your hand on the leash. Substitute this "pull-up" method wherever it is indicated that you "push down" on the leash. It may be necessary to switch from left to right hand when using this "pull-up" method. Everything else remains the same as described before.

A word of caution. If your dog is overly aggressive, temperamental, or a "fear biter" excessive force will make him bite or react in a hostile manner, such as with deep throat growls. If this is the situation then the "pull-up" method is definitely out, no matter how big the animal. The "push-down" method may be too dangerous as well. Use the front-paw method exclusively. Even at that it will have to be done gently and with great patience. Instead of pulling his paws out in front of him, gently and slowly push his front paws from behind until he slumps to the ground, grudgingly, but without aggressive resistance. Give the voice command "DOWWWWW-wwwn" as you push his paws and coax him soothingly. It's like the old conundrum, "Where does a five-hundred-pound pussycat sleep? Anywhere he wants!" If it still does not work, then avoid this command or engage the services of a professional trainer. This problem will not arise with a young dog or puppy. It only happens with older dogs who have had enough time to develop bad habits or nervous, neurotic behavior caused by too little training given too late.

DEFINITION OF "DOWN-STAY"

The dog is on the ground, head erect, eyes looking forward. The front legs are extended and the hind quarters relaxed with the rear weight resting on one haunch or the other. He remains in that position until he is released by the person who placed him there. (See Fig. 18.)

FIGURE 18.
"Down" and "Down-Stay." These are the various ways a dog may position himself while in "Down-Stay." The Weimaraner and the Maltese are in perfect position. The Husky has found his own variation of the position.

PROCEDURE AND TECHNIQUE FOR THE "DOWN-STAY"

If the dog has learned the "Sit-Stay," then it is simply a matter of using the same technique for the "Down-Stay."

After placing him in the "Down" give the command "Stay" in a firm voice. Because it is not an action command do not use his name before or afterward. Upon giving the command, flatten your left hand with fingers close together as for a salute and place it in front of his eyes. Your hand should be four inches in front of them. The hand signal is given simultaneously with the voice command. It is a deliberate but quick gesture which temporarily blocks the dog's vision. Assuming the animal has been taught the "Sit-Stay," that's all there is to be done. If he does not respond properly, then review the chapter dealing with "Sit-Stay" and give the dog a few brush-up lessons.

One last note. The commands "Down" and "Stay" are not corrections. If the dog jumps up on a stranger, the couch, the bed, the dinner table, or into the cat's litter box do not yell "Down" and expect him to respond properly. He will become confused. A firm "No" is the only way to make a correction. From there you can employ any command you wish. "Down" will do very well.

11 / "Come When Called"

The dog's name prefixed to the word "Come"is all that's necessary in getting the animal to "Come When Called." As pointed out earlier, language is not your dog's *forte*. Adding "Okay" to "Silver, come" gives a note of good cheer and reassurance that you're not angry with him. Anything more than that will louse up the command and draw a blank in the dog's mind. "Okay, Silver, come," is all it really takes, once the dog has been taught the command. More than that adds confusion, uncertainty, and a lack of response.

There are two cautions concerning this command. The first has to do with older dogs. "Come When Called" must be considered for puppies and young dogs only. The second has to do with the indoor-outdoor use of the command. If your dog lives in the city it is extremely hazardous to allow the dog off the leash. Therefore, consider it very carefully before teaching "Come When Called" out of the house. it could result in the death of the animal. On the other hand, using the command indoors is very practical and offers a convenient way to get the dog to where you want him to be.

DEFINITION OF "COME WHEN CALLED"

The dog comes to you when you call him and goes into a "Sit" position in front of you, regardless of any distractions. (See Fig. 19.)

FIGURE 19.
"Come When Called." Give the verbal command and hand signal and pull the leash toward you. Use both hands, one after the other. The dog sits when he reaches you.

BENEATH THE SURFACE
OF THE TRAINING

This is probably the command that people want most and
have the least idea how to execute. It makes the greatest
demand of the dog. Most of his life is spent playing and pur-
suing all distractions that cross his path. Now he is being
asked to respond immediately by shifting his focus and using
all his concentration to please you. When a dog is indoors
there is nothing for him to do but come when you call him.
But when he is outside there are smells, sights, other dogs,
children, people, moving objects, and noises that command
his attention. To get him to resist all that and obey your
command is quite a chore.

In order to teach him to come to you when he's *off-leash*
it is necessary to start by teaching him *on-leash*. There is no
way to teach this command without starting on-leash. Before
getting him trained off-leash you must go through a training
process of gradually extending the length of the leash. *Never
try this command off-leash until he is obeying perfectly on-
leash.* It is too dangerous.

The most important rule to remember is *never* to call the
dog to you in order to reprimand him. If you use his name or
the command "Come" and then correct or punish him he
will never come to you again. Avoid statements like "Princess,

come. What did you do? Shame, shame! Don't you ever do that again!" Some people even go further by hitting the dog after he has obeyed the command. Each command must be dealt with individually. If the dog obeys a command, praise him. If he "Comes When Called" it is a betrayal of the rules if you scold him. Besides, using his name for correction will only make him associate the sound of his name with "Uh oh. Here it comes." No one in his right mind will run enthusiastically to get hollered at or punished. If the dog needs correction for an infraction of the rules *you must go to him to do it*. In that way his ability to "Come When Called" will not be impaired. A dog should feel that coming to you is a good thing. He should always feel confident that it is a pleasant experience. This attitude is achieved by lavishing him with praise every time he obeys. If you are consistent, he will always come to you.

It is important in teaching this command that the dog never get into the habit of hesitating when called. He should respond immediately. His reward for coming is the praise, but it should be established from the beginning that he must come on the first command. His immediate response could be important to his safety in the city. More dogs are killed in the city by automobiles than by natural causes. This consideration alone makes the command a very valuable one.

PROCEDURE AND TECHNIQUE FOR "COME WHEN CALLED" —ON-LEASH

Begin indoors or out. An area that offers a few distractions is not objectionable as a training place. Use the six-foot leash. First put the dog through his basic commands, i.e., "Heel," "Sit," "Sit-Stay," "Down," "Down-Stay," etc. Then put him in "Sit-Stay." Begin the lesson facing the dog.

Place yourself in front of the dog slightly less than the full extent of the six-foot leash. Holding the leash with the left hand (thumb in loop as described in previous chapters), allow a very slight amount of slack so there is no chance of pulling the dog forward. With the slightest tug the dog will walk toward you and that is undesirable without a command. Keep the leash hand (the left) slightly above the waist for greater control of the dog.

The next thing to do is employ the voice command. It is

important that the tone of voice indicate to the dog that coming to you is one of the most exciting, fun things he could do. The dog should be happy coming to you because he's going to get a tremendous amount of praise. Because this is an action command, employ the dog's name as a prefix to the command "Come." However, use the expletive "Okay" before his name. The command, therefore, sounds like this: "*Okay,* Princess, come!" The "Okay" should be delivered in a very cheerful, upbeat tone of voice. Try to communicate your affection. Never sound harsh or stern. Accentuate the "Okay" and let the "Princess, come" trail along. The dog should start moving on the "Okay." It is quite possible that in the past, the traditional squeaking of the lips sound was made to get the dog to come. You know the sound, the one that's like a squeezed balloon. Lip squeaking and whistling are poor substitutes for a definite command. Very few of us can whistle or squeak loud enough if the dog is in the middle of the street with the distraction of traffic or other outdoor noises.

It is quite possible that the dog will come on the first try. If he does, be sure to reward him with lavish praise. It is not important, at this point, that he sit once he gets to you. If he jumps on you the first few times it's quite understandable. *Do not correct him when he is being taught a new thing.* He may always associate "coming" with the correction and the command is shot forever. He can always be corrected at another time, after he has learned the command properly.

Tugging the leash. Once little Kitszi starts coming to you freely, extend the leash hand and give a gentle tug on the word "Okay." Always tug the leash on the word "Okay." The sequence is: "Okay" (gently tug the leash) "Waldo, come." (He comes to you.) "That's a good fella!" As soon as he comes to you give him his praise. Make it very exciting for him. We emphasize the praise in this command because later you will be competing with very great distractions, and the only way to overcome them is to motivate the dog properly. That can only be done with praise.

The hand signal. The next step is to teach the dog the hand signal that accompanies the voice command. This is very useful if the dog is a great distance away. The hand signal is a natural, logical gesture that should feel very comfortable. It is simply a matter of moving your right hand upward from the side of your body and swinging it around toward your left shoulder. (See Fig. 20.) This gesture is used by humans for the same purpose. The sequence becomes: "Okay." (Tug the leash with your left hand. Swing your right hand around, making a complete gesture.) "Melba, come." Give her a lot of praise when she gets to you.

Going into the "Sit" position after "Coming When Called." After the command is given, pull in the leash—using both hands, one after another—until the entire leash is in and the dog has no choice but to sit when he gets to you. In order

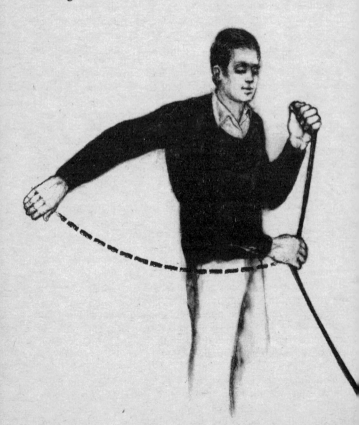

FIGURE 20. *Proper hand signal for "Come When Called."*

to help it along, pull up on the leash once he is at your feet and give the command "Sit." This sequence is: "Okay." (Tug the leash with your left hand. Swing your right hand around, making a complete gesture, *but grab the leash this time.*) "Pete, come." (Pull in the leash, using both hands.) "Good boy, good boy." (By now you have pulled him gently to your feet. Raise the leash with your left hand.) "Sit. Good boy. That's a good boy."

The animal is taught to sit when he gets to you for a couple of very practical reasons. First of all, when he responds to the command "Come" he will start running to you. If he is some distance away it is quite possible that he will crash into you at about forty miles an hour, knocking you off your feet. Or he may shoot right by in his inability to stop. If he is conditioned to sit when he gets to you, he will automatically slow down as he approaches. Repeat these techniques ten or fifteen times or until he responds properly. Remember, all of this is done *on-leash.* At no time should you try it without the leash. The most important reason is safety. But another reason is for control so that he can be guided if he starts veering left or right. To increase the distance for him to come, simply back up as he approaches you. Give him encouragement as he walks toward you. It helps to hold his attention and also motivates him for future commands. "Okay, Pete, come. Pete, come. Okay. Good boy. Good fella." Once he gets to you, "Sit." "Good boy."

"COME WHEN CALLED"—OFF-LEASH

To teach this command off-leash, outdoors, one must be prepared to spend several months at it. It is not recommended for city dogs. But if you have lots of acreage or access to a fenced-off park or field, it can be done with no danger. You should be cautioned that in order to be successful with this off-leash command you must start with a young dog or puppy. Once a dog is six months or older it is almost impossible.

Start by teaching him to come from a ten-foot distance. Do not drop the leash and walk away thinking the dog will stay there until he is called. Obtain a fifty-foot clothesline and hook it to the loop of his leash. With the six-foot leash you had total control of the animal. At ten, fifteen, twenty, twenty-five feet, or more you are not going to have the same amount of control. Start off by using the same *on-leash* technique as before, but this time allow ten feet of leash. Once the dog has performed perfectly at ten feet, go back to the six-foot distance and then back to ten. The repetition reinforces the learning process so he'll never forget what he's been taught. Obviously it cannot be done in one session. It will take two, three, or four lessons for the six-foot technique alone.

Extending the length of the leash. If the dog is responding perfectly to the ten-foot distance, extend the leash to fifteen feet. At this distance you will not be able to reel in the leash as quickly as he can run to you. But if he comes to you at ten feet, then reeling it in hand over hand is no longer necessary. The theory is that if he'll come at ten feet perfectly, then he'll come at twenty or even forty feet. It's then a matter of practice. After the six-foot technique is perfect, go to ten feet, fifteen, twenty, twenty-five, thirty, thirty-five, etc.

Correction from a long distance. The purpose of always having the clothesline tied to the leash is to have some control of the dog, even if he cannot be reeled in as on the six-foot leash. Suppose you are training him at twenty feet and the dog is coming toward you. All of a sudden he spots another dog at fifteen feet and bolts. Without the line on him that would be the end of the session. But what can be done is to lift up the line and hold it tightly. When he reaches the end of the rope he will be stopped cold. At that instant yell "No!" The correction will be a shocking surprise, one that he will not forget. The point is that even at thirty or forty feet you still have the ability to correct him if he bolts. This, incidentally, is a common occurrence and will happen many times. Continue the technique until the dog is responding perfectly at fifty feet. At this point it is time to try him without the clothesline.

Without the clothesline. It is possible that the dog has, all along, recognized that the leash is on and he has to obey. But what happens once the leash is removed? He may recognize the difference. It is for this reason that you are working in an enclosed area. If he runs away, *do not panic. Do not run after him.* If you do, he'll dart away. The thing to do is run in the opposite direction saying, "Come on, boy." He'll follow because it will seem like a game. If that doesn't work, get down on your hands and knees and cheerfully entice him to come to you. Once he is back in your control do not reprimand him if he has responded to your entreaties. If you do he will never respond to them again. Once he comes to you, even if it took half an hour, praise him for it. Never correct a dog when he comes to you. That is why this command requires a great deal of patience.

If the dog does not come off-leash after having worked up to the fifty feet of clothesline, it means starting again at six feet. Of course you will be able to move from distance to distance at a much more rapid pace. It is safe to assume that the dog has learned the command but only associates it with the leash. At this juncture the formula: command, correction, praise is brought to bear. Give the command. "Okay, Pete, come." If the dog doesn't come when called, give him a correction, "No!" This should get him going. When he gets to you, give him his praise. In this manner proceed from distance to distance until you have reached fifty feet. When you try him off-leash this time make sure there are absolutely no distractions. Give him every opportunity to perform properly. He will always obey the command if it is enforced properly. Once he is coming when called off-leash, without distractions, try when there are distractions. You may be pleasantly surprised.

Never use the command "Come" in a harsh tone of voice and never reprimand the dog after he has obeyed the command. This carries over into the home as well as outdoors and during the training sessions. If the dog chews something in the living room and you call him in from the kitchen in order to scold or correct him, you will be destroying the value of this command. In your everyday usage of these commands you will reinforce the training if you execute these techniques properly.

12 / "Go to Your Place"

Unlike humans, dogs do not feel insulted if you put them in their place. As a matter of fact, it is a blessing for them to know where to be in order to stay out from underfoot. Dogs are not immune to the frustrations of trying to please an indecisive and inconsistent colleague.

Although "Go to Your Place" is useful for people who live in a full-size house, it is manna from heaven for the city apartment dweller. The average apartment has a bedroom, living room, and kitchen. When the apartment dweller is trying to prepare dinner for a small dinner party, the dog is usually driven mad trying to keep out of the way. If he settles at your feet in the kitchen, he is scolded and told to go into the living room. Once he settles in the living room, he has to dodge the dust mop and avoid being sucked up by the vacuum cleaner. By this time he has been yelled at seventeen times and he's just about ready to steal several caviar canapes (dogs love caviar), which will evoke a shrill hysterical scream from the belabored epicure. The dog is then locked in the bathroom for the evening until a guest uses it and passes out in fright. In the meantime the dog is suffering from boredom and claustrophobia with a pinch of paranoia thrown in for good measure . Of course the hosts are nervous and on edge and ready to give the dog to the first farmer who says he can use him to bite cows. Thus ends another potentially happy relationship between dog and owner. It's too bad, because all this can so easily be avoided with the command "Go to Your Place."

DEFINITION OF "GO TO YOUR PLACE"

At your command the dog stops whatever he is doing and leaves wherever he is doing it, goes to a designated place, and stays there for an indefinite time.

BENEATH THE SURFACE
OF THE TRAINING

The dog should have an out-of-the-way area that is designated as his little corner of the world. The area should be carefully selected so that at no time is he in anyone's way or in danger of being forced to move once he's placed there. It is especially considerate if the area is not too removed from the activities of the family. Dogs get vicarious pleasure from merely watching the evening's entertainment. An added benefit from this command is that it ends begging for food once you have sat down to dinner.

One of the ways to enhance the training is to place his toys, playthings, and bones in his designated area. He will feel quite at home and much more secure. Give him a small piece of carpet or an old cushion in order to make his area cozy and comfortable. Once all this is established the dog will be in a much better frame of mind. Psychologically, it is very important for his well-being.

In a household where there is more than one animal, this designation of territory is very important. If there are two male dogs, for instance, there is a constant competition for territorial rights. In this situation, designate a place for each animal and never violate the established territorial rights of each respective dog. With a cat and a dog, never let the cat use the dog's area for anything. In the case of a male and a female dog when the latter goes in heat there is very little that territory can do to avoid contact. The dogs must be kept apart (assuming you don't want them to mate) in more practical ways. Outside of a mating situation, the animals will quickly learn to respect each other's territorial rights.

This command offers the owner a firm control over the animal's behavior at very important times. If a friend or neighbor enters the home and does not want to be annoyed with the dog's demand for attention, simply tell him to go to his place and that's the end of it. This goes back to the time of the caveman when the dog stayed outside as a guard. That was his place.

It is helpful to understand that the dog will always go to his place on command if it is not made to seem like a punishment. Even though your motive is to get the dog out of mischief, always give the command on an upbeat so that he does not feel that something bad is connected with going to his place.

It is not to be equated with "Go to your room," an expression that many a parent has used on an errant child.

PROCEDURE AND TECHNIQUE FOR "GO TO YOUR PLACE"

The first step in teaching this command is to select a permanent spot that will be used exclusively by the dog as the one place where he can go and never be in the way.

Starting at five feet. In teaching the lesson, use the standard six-foot leash and choke collar. Because this is an action command, always use his name first. Start out five feet away from the designated place and say, "Pete, go to your place." Then commence to walk the dog to the spot. Once you get him there, give the command "Sit." Praise him. Then give him the command "Down" and, finally, "Stay." Praise him. Leave him there as you walk six feet away. Do not leave his vision. He will probably stay, provided you're in the room. Assuming the dog has learned "Come When Called," call him to you. Repeat this procedure fifteen times.

The command "Go to Your Place" should be given in a pleasant and gentle tone of voice. Even though learning is hard work for a dog, make him feel that this is a pleasant command, one which he will enjoy. However, do not lose the firm, authoritative sound that you have developed. Add a happy quality to it.

Once the dog willingly accompanies you to his place from five feet, try it at ten feet. Again, get his attention with, "Pete, go to your place." Walk him to the spot. Place him in "Sit." Place him in "Down" and then "Stay." Walk six feet away and after a few seconds call him. Repeat the whole thing several times. Don't be surprised if he starts leading you to his place once he's been doing it a few times. This is a happy experience for him. He gets a lot of praise and affection for doing it properly. Do not, however, become too lax during the training period. If he starts sniffing something on the way to his place, exercise firm leash control. Direct him to the exact location of his place. Nothing must stand in the way once you have given the command.

Extending the distance. Take a twenty-foot clothesline and tie it to the loop of the dog's leash. Stand back the full distance of the line and give the command, "Pete, go to your place." Let him do it by himself. The reason for tying a line to him is control. If he veers away from his place, correct him, say "No" and then repeat the original command. If he gets confused or decides not to do it, walk him there as before. The command, unlike some of the others, involves more teaching than discipline.

Other rooms. The next step is to teach him this command from other rooms. Using the six-foot leash repeat the procedure, but this time from another room at a greater distance. Try it several times from every room in your apartment or house. You will actually be teaching him the path to his place from every part of your quarters and it will be permanently printed in his brain. The toughest room for him will probably be the bedroom because it is usually the farthest. But once he learns that, he will know the command perfectly. Once the dog knows this command on-leash it is guaranteed that he'll be able to do it off-leash.

A word of caution. Do not give this command promiscuously. Do not make it a family joke or something with which to impress friends and neighbors. Only use the command as it's needed. If he has to go to his place every five minutes it's going to make him crazy. Let him enjoy going to his place. Let him consider it his little haven when things get difficult. He will soon be going there without the command. He'll probably pick that area to stay for most of the day. That will be his little indoor doghouse. A home within a home.

Now that you have successfully completed the last twelve chapters, you may consider your dog obedience-trained. Congratulations! Both you and your dog deserve a biscuit.

The next part of the book is more or less graduate work. Now that your dog is obedience-trained, you may tackle his individual problems as outlined in "Puppy and Mature Problems," "Mature Problems Only," and "Problem Dogs." The first twelve chapters have given you a basis from which to work.

PART II

After The
Obedience Course

Fortunately for us, dogs do not respond to Freudian analysis, touch therapy, or any other form of psychotherapy. If they did there would probably be a stampede to dog "shrinks" and sniff-touch encounter-group studios. It would create a new set of economics in an already costly pet market.

In this chapter a great deal of territory is covered in an attempt to give some useful information concerning the dozens of behavioral problems that occur in dogs. Selected here are those that come up the most often, but no doubt others will be overlooked owing to the limitations of space or technical/medical information available. Many of these problems never arise because a successfully completed obedience course, such as the one outlined in this book, was initiated. Many of these problems can be diminished in degree simply by going over various aspects of the obedience course. A well-trained and disciplined dog will not eat up the carpet, bark excessively, bite, etc. However, inadvertent environmental factors sometimes play a destructive part in creating those annoying bad habits that dogs very often acquire. For example, a family that goes to work every day, leaving the dog alone, may come home to a destroyed couch, never knowing that the phone rang continuously, putting the dog into a mad frenzy. Incorrect discipline is the main cause of these problems and tends to worsen them as long as it is continued. Punishments, scoldings, temper tantrums, beatings all tend to create problems and worsen those that already exist.

Besides continuous brushups on the obedience course, we suggest that you try to think through a dog's situation from his perspective. Like a psychologist, one can often solve a problem by understanding its cause. You would then be in a position to change or remove those factors that are upsetting the dog and making him behave the way he does. Teasing, roughhouse play, abuse from children, chaining him down, overexcitement are but a few of those factors that may be at the root of the problem. Some dogs will not respond to the suggestions made in this chapter and will require the long, tedious kind of attention that only a professional trainer can provide. If you love your dog and want to keep him, it is best to take this final but effective step. A good trainer not only has the technical facility to handle most dog problems, but is emotionally uninvolved, thus giving him the needed patience that underlies all good animal handling. It is like the difference between an aspirin and a doctor's prescription.

The first two chapters in this part, "Puppy and Mature Problems" and "Mature Problems Only," describe problems and their solutions. These are all measures that any dog owner can take and experience good results with. The last chapter, "Problem Dogs," does not offer any such measures that the owner can take himself. These are problems that only a trainer can solve. What we do offer is an aid to recognition of these problems so that the owner can take the proper steps in obtaining professional assistance.

13 / Puppy and Mature Problems

BEGGING

This is a problem that starts out in puppyhood as a cute stunt and winds up as an obnoxious annoyance in mature life. There is nothing worse than a dog sitting next to you at the dinner table, looking up, and whining for food. Although barely tolerable when it's just a daily family dinner, it is completely unacceptable when you are entertaining guests. It can ruin an otherwise pleasant social occasion.

Obviously, this is a habit that is formed when the dog is very young, and once again the owner is to blame. When you give the dog snacks and between-meal treats, you are on the way to teaching him to beg. He begins to expect food at any time of the day or night and never learns that his feeding time is the main meal of the day. He has learned that his eating area is anywhere that you are dealing with food. As in the section "Taking Food from the Table," make it a firm rule never to feed him anywhere but in his bowl, in its regular place. Also, never give him anything except his own food, *at his regular feeding time only*.

In order to break him of his begging habit, start placing the leash and collar on him before dinner. Sit down to dinner and wait for him to make his move. The instant he starts begging from anyone, give him a hard corrective jerk accompanied by a loud "No." Tell everyone at the table what is about to happen so it doesn't upset them and ruin their meal. Alternatives to this method are: Use of the "throw can" accompanied with a firm "No"; the command "Down" and "Stay"; and the command "Go to Your Place." If you do it consistently he will stop this nasty little habit in short order.

CHEWING

Chewing is one of the most expensive and destructive problems that any dog owner faces. We are talking about chewing furniture, curtains, draperies, appliances, baseboards, shoes, clothing, etc. Owners have lost hundreds and sometimes thousands of dollars in damage. Very often chewing has been the cause of failure in owner-animal relations and has resulted in a parting of the ways. For the owner it ends in frustration, but for the dog, it means an uncertain future in terms of his mortality. It's sad because there is no excuse for the problem, inasmuch as it is readily solvable.

There are several solutions. Some dogs will respond favorably to any one of the many sprays on the market. You spray the items that the dog has chewed and tends to go back to. Some sprays are unpleasant to the dog's sense of smell while others are unpleasant to taste. An alternative is to use alum, a powder that can be purchased inexpensively in any drugstore. Mix it with a small amount of water, make it into a paste, and smear it on the dog's favorite chewing spots. The mixture tastes bitter and is extremely unpleasant for the animal. Although alum is not harmful if ingested, it should be used in small quantities. Alum is used medicinally as an astringent and a styptic and could upset the dog if he swallowed a large quantity. However, that is not likely to happen owing to its unpleasant taste. Tobasco or hot sauce is also effective.

Some people have had success merely by playing the radio during the time they are not at home (when most chewing takes place). Others have made one- or two-hour tape recordings of conversation, which tends to make the dog uncertain about the owner's presence. "His master's voice" can be effective because dogs rarely chew when the owner is home. Record one or two hours of conversation with an intermittent correction. In other words, yell "No" and shake a "throw can" every five minutes during the first twenty minutes of the tape recording.

If the dog's favorite chewing object is a couch cover or bolster or bed pillow, the mousetrap technique will certainly end the problem. (See "Jumping on Furniture.")

When the chewing problem pertains to a puppy, stay alert to which objects the animal is chewing and discourage it immediately before it develops into an adult habit. Discourage him from going after wooden objects or anything at all that might resemble furniture, clothing, carpeting, curtains, or anything you value. A rawhide toy that he can call his own is the safest preventative you can employ to avoid a destructive behavior problem. Do not wait until it is too late and you have lost your valuable carpeting. A puppy's chewing problem is usually because of teething. When you leave the house leave several ice cubes around for the dog. The coldness will numb his gums and ease the pain. An alternative is to soak a wash-cloth in cold water and freeze it. This will serve the same purpose as the ice cubes.

Many adult dogs chew when left alone because they are bored, frightened, nervous, or insecure about whether or not you will return. They do not do it as a spiteful act. Punish-ment is counterproductive and changes nothing except to add to the dog's insecurity. If you can make a determination as to why he chews, you might be able to change the conditions of his environment and correct the problem. For example: take the phone off the hook if the bell frightens him, do not leave him alone for too long a period of time (have a friend look in on him), get him a cat for a playmate, leave plenty of rawhide toys or bones, etc. With careful deliberation every problem can be solved.

EXCESSIVE BARKING

There are two aspects to the problem of excessive barking. The first is when the dog barks while the owner is home, and that is usually caused by a doorbell ringing, noise outside the door, a stranger at the door, a desire for food, a desire to go out, etc. The second aspect is when the owner is not home. The owner comes home from work or shopping and finds an angry note from a neighbor or landlord to stop the dog from barking or else face the legal consequences.

Solving the barking problem when the owner is home is much easier than when the owner is not at home. By leaving the leash and choke collar on the dog you are prepared to deliver a corrective jerk and a firm "No" when the dog barks. Even shaking the "throw can" and saying "No" often works. But the corrective jerk is the most effective method.

If the dog barks excessively when no one is home, the solu-tion lies in the basic obedience course. There are many rea-sons why a dog will bark when he is left alone. He may be undisciplined; he may hear a lot of noises outside; he simply may want his own way, i.e., to have you walk through the door and play with him. Basic obedience lessons tend to calm him down, reassure him, make him responsive. The more responsive the dog is to you, the more eager he is to please. If the dog has had no basic obedience lessons this is the time to start. If he has had lessons then simply go over three or four commands as a refresher. Run him through his paces, so to speak, and remind him of his training. Don't forget to praise him every time he performs properly.

If that doesn't work, then try leaving the house and waiting outside. Do everything you normally do when you leave. Follow the established routine, such as putting out certain lights, closing the curtains, etc. Do not lock the door. Be sure to leave his leash and collar on. Pretend to leave the house and do not stand so close to the door that the dog can smell your presence. He must be convinced that you have really left the house. When he starts to bark, run in, grab his leash, and execute a hard corrective jerk accompanied by an angry "No!" If you do this three or four times with very firm corrections (jerking hard enough to lift him off the ground) he will understand exactly what you want him not to do. Praise him afterward for having stopped barking. This is a problem that must be solved, because it can result in having to get rid of the dog or finding yourself evicted from your house or apartment. A very hard corrective jerk is recommended if it's going to work. It's much more humane in the long run than having to surrender the dog to an unknown home or institution.

You may run into the problem of his not barking for an hour after you leave. One way to solve this is with the use of a one- or two-hour tape recording of family conversation with an intermittent correction. Yell "No" and shake a "throw can" every five minutes for the first twenty minutes of the recording. If he suspects that you are around, he will not bark. An alternative is to wait out the hour outside the house on a weekend when you can spare the time, and use the corrective jerk as outlined above. But in either case the problem must be dealt with before it is too late.

In all these suggested methods you must always accompany your action with a firm "No" and then praise after he responds properly. In a short while you will only have to use a firm "No."

EXCESSIVE WETTING

Holding his urine is one of the primary requisites for a domesticated pet. But many dogs tend to release it in small quantities at the most peculiar moments and sometimes trail it all over the house. There are several explanations. It can be a symptom of sickness, disease, or injury to the kidneys and bladder. It doesn't hurt to have your dog checked by a veterinarian. Assuming the dog is in good health, wetting can be an indication of a very shy or timid dog. A dog of this temperament will "piddle" when he is punished or yelled at. He wets from fear or perhaps excitement. Urinating is an instinctual act of submission to the domination of another animal and is a direct parallel to excessive authority from the dog's master. When a male puppy is confronted with a mature dog of the same gender a ritual takes place. They determine each other's sex by sniffing and then decide who will prevail in the situation. There is usually a brief, physical encounter with the puppy or young dog losing the battle and indicating his submission by rolling over on his back and urinating. It is his way of acknowledging the older male's superiority. The identical interaction occurs between you and your dog when you punish him or yell at him and he urinates.

One way to cope with it is to be much more gentle than usual and to eliminate punishments and scoldings. Do not use threatening gestures or sudden movements. A limited water intake can help reduce the problem. Weaning the dog away from his shy or timid temperament will eventually end the problem. (See "The Shy Dog.")

GOING INTO THE GARBAGE

Unless it has already happened to you, this problem seems to be one of those endearing little habits that make such good anecdote material for people who enjoy talking about their dogs. In our opinion this nasty little trait is not only disgusting but has all the potential for costing the owner a great deal of money. More than once a dog has ripped into the garbage sack and scattered it all over the house. In addition, the little devil chewed up much of it and ingested such savories as eggshells, coffee grounds, etc. The dog then moved into the living room and regurgitated all over the two-hundred-year-old Persian rug. To come home to that is to experience the first emotions of *dogicide*. Of course, if the dog happens to split a few hollow chicken bones with his teeth and then swallows the jagged ends you might come home to find a dead dog. Going into the garbage can be serious.

This problem arises whether you are home or away. Because of the powerful smell, animals are extremely attracted to this symphony of scents. Obviously, the easiest way to solve the problem is to simply not leave the garbage pail around, especially if you go out. But that doesn't really teach the dog anything. Set up a simulated situation. Place the leash and collar on the dog and purposely open the lid to the garbage pail. Walk away. The minute the dog sticks his nose in the pail give him a hard corrective jerk and a very loud "No." *Then praise him.* You may also try shaking the "throw can" if it's more convenient. You should get good results if you repeat this technique four or five times. In the event that you are leaving the house sprinkle Tabasco sauce or hot Chinese mustard on top of the garbage. This is an object lesson that really works.

JUMPING ON FURNITURE

This is another undesirable characteristic of many dogs, both young and old alike. It comes from poor discipline on the part of the owner who allows the habit to develop. If the dog is allowed to sleep with his owner in the bed, it is very logical for him to assume that the chairs and sofas are merely an extension of the bed. Furniture is furniture and the dog makes no distinctions. Therefore, the question must be asked: is the dog allowed to jump on the furniture or not?

There are several solutions to the problem. If the dog is still a puppy the "throw can" is very effective. Wait for the animal to jump on the furniture. The minute he does, you shake the can and say "No" in a firm voice. Do not throw the can as you might with an older dog. You do not want to scare the young puppy. As you are aware by now, the "throw can" solves a multitude of problems. Do not forget to praise the dog immediately after he responds to the correction.

In the case of an older dog, apply the same technique with this exception: *throw* the can. Of course it is not suggested that you throw the can directly at him. Throw it to the side. Because the dog is older, it takes a little more than shaking the can to startle him. Once again say "No" with a firm voice and then praise the animal after he responds.

In the event that the "throw can" method does not work, it is suggested you use the leash and choke collar. When you are home leave the leash on until he jumps on the furniture. As he does, give him a very firm corrective jerk accompanied by a stern "No." As soon as he stops jumping give him his praise. Remember, without the praise the correction is meaningless.

A very upsetting aspect to this problem is when the dog waits for you to leave the house before he jumps up on the sofa or whatever his favorite spot is. (You can be sure he has one.) Do you come home and discover fur, saliva, or worse on your expensive bedspread or brocade slipcover? If so, it indicates that the dog waits for you to leave, commits his crime, and scoots off the minute he hears you coming. One answer is to tape record one or two hours of conversation with an intermittent correction. Every five minutes yell "No" and shake a "throw can" for the first twenty minutes of the recording.

Another solution to this problem sounds awful, but in reality is painless and quite humane. Set ten or fifteen small mousetraps over the couch or bed and cover them with five or six thicknesses of newspaper. Tape the paper thoroughly so that the dog cannot hurt himself. When you leave, the dog is probably going to jump on the couch and set the traps off. The traps will hit the newspaper with a loud noise and startle him. This works almost every time. Repeat the technique until you come home to find that the traps have not been set off.

It is important to remember that dogs are taught to jump on furniture. If they are not allowed to do it at any time then they won't. Most people think it's cute to cradle a puppy in their arms and sit on the couch with it. There is no difference between a puppy sitting directly on the couch or sitting in your arms with you seated on the couch. That is the beginning of your problem and that's the time to nip it in the bud. Remember, it ceases to be cute when the dog is full grown and the habit firmly established. Allowing the dog to sleep in your bed is also an open invitation to jumping on the furniture. The choice is yours.

JUMPING ON PEOPLE

Almost any dog will jump up on people if he is excited, happy, and untrained. This happens on the street and in the house when someone comes to visit. The animal usually wants to play and get some attention. The biggest problem connected with it is the behavior of the owner. If the puppy or the dog is not supposed to jump up on people, then that rule must apply in every situation. You cannot have the dog jump up on you when you feel playful and then expect him not to do it when you are no longer in the mood. It is too confusing for him. Consistency is the only sure cure. In most cases where this problem exists you will find that the owner encourages the dog to jump up once or twice a week. The rest of the time the owner does not like it and yells at the dog when he jumps. It is precisely because of this inconsistency that the dog jumps on anyone who pays the slightest attention to him. One must answer the question: do you want him to jump on you or not?

If the answer is no, then a correction (the corrective jerk and a firm "No") will stop him in most cases, providing that you maintain that attitude. (See Fig. 21.) If you give in just once you will destroy the training. If you teach a puppy not to jump by correcting him when he tries it, he will never do it unless you permit him that one time.

Puppies can be taught with the use of a "throw can." (See "Equipment.") Whenever the puppy tries to jump or climb up on you or anyone else, shake the can vigorously and say "No" in a very firm tone of voice. Do not scare the little dog, simply command his attention and impress upon him that this behavior is displeasing. Once you have made the correction and he responds properly, then give him affectionate praise. Do not bend over and pet him or he'll jump again. Tell him he's a good dog in a friendly voice. He will soon understand that he doesn't have to jump to get your love.

In the case of a grown dog who has been indulging in this behavior for a while, use a different technique that's based on the same principle. Arrange for a relative to have the dog on leash and choke collar before you come home. When you walk in the door and the dog makes a jump, the person holding the leash gives him a corrective jerk and a very firm "No." Assuming the dog has been obedience-trained, he should be commanded to "Sit" immediately following the correction. Give him his praise after he obeys the command. If the dog

FIGURE 21.
Jumping on people. Employ the corrective jerk. Wait until the dog is standing on two legs before executing the correction.

has not yet been obedience-trained, then the corrective jerk must be done with vigor as you pull to the right side. He may still try to jump after the first jerk. Simply do it again until he stops. If this process is repeated several times in one evening you will be surprised at the results.

If the infraction occurs outside on a stranger or anyone else, do not merely pull him away. Give him a corrective jerk to the right and walk in the opposite direction. This jerk will cause the dog enough discomfort to discourage him from trying it again. Do it every time he jumps up and you will solve the problem. But remember, if you or anyone else encourages the dog to jump up this training will have no effect. You must inform everyone who comes in contact with the dog that they must not give the animal any invitations.

No cruel or excessively harsh techniques that have been used in the past are recommended, such as kneeing the dog in the chest or stepping on his toes. These painful techniques are not necessary if you remember to be consistent in your demands.

NIPPING

All puppies have a teething problem, as do all infants. Because teething is painful, puppies bite or nip to ease the pressure of the incoming teeth. They will bite hands, fingers, toys, and furniture. Sometimes they are encouraged to bite if the owner makes a habit of placing his hand in the animal's mouth when playing. This is like teaching the dog to bite. There are several ways to ease this situation. One method is to soak a washcloth in cold water and place it in the freezing unit of the refrigerator. When it is frozen give it to the dog to chew. The coldness will numb his gums and relieve the pain. Consequently, he will not bite as much as he did. Quite often this is done with babies by refrigerating their teething rings.

Another approach to the problem is to give the puppy a rawhide or synthetic toy. It is not suggested that the dog be given an old discarded shoe or sock. You will be sorry later. The dog will not be able to distinguish between an old shoe and a new one. The rawhide toys may be used in conjunction with the frozen washcloth.

It is important to solve the nipping problem early in the dog's life because it can lead to a serious biting problem later.

The puppy should always be discouraged from nipping at your fingers or anything else. It is better to substitute a rawhide toy for your fingers than to inflict a harsh punishment or scolding. All the yelling, hitting, or finger-pointing in the world is not going to stop the dog's teeth from growing and giving him pain. And if you scare the dog when he is a young puppy he may grow shy or aggressive and then you will have a biting problem that is much more difficult to solve.

RUNNING OUT OF THE HOUSE

This is a problem that could mean life or death for the dog. If he runs out the door and into the street he could be struck by a car, and good-bye dog. Most dog owners have either had this problem or are still experiencing it. Even though a dog has had some form of basic obedience course and has been taught the "Sit-Stay," he will still attempt to run out the front door if given half a chance. The reason is simple. Going through the front door represents a happy experience to the dog. It is through that door that he is taken outside to play, to relieve himself, to see children and other animals. Obviously, he is primed at a second's notice to go dashing out to the never-never land of fun and games. He must be taught that he can only go through the door when given permission.

In order to break him of this habit, set up an artificial situation so he can be corrected when he tries to run out. Put his choke collar and training leash on and keep it in hand. Prearrange to have someone ring the doorbell. Place the dog in "Sit-Stay." Tell the person to come in. The door should open and be left open. When the dog bolts for the door give him an extremely hard corrective jerk, shout "No," and turn around and walk the other way. Then place him in "Sit-Stay" again. Naturally, the dog must be taught "Sit-Stay" in order to do this. Every time the doorbell rings he should be placed in "Sit-Stay." Repeat the procedure several times a day until he no longer tries to run out. It may take a few days but it's well worth the effort.

In practicing make sure you maintain absolute control of the dog. He may not respond properly at first and if you do not keep a firm grip on the leash he will run out. Do not lose the dog in the process of teaching him. Any time he makes a lunge for the door give him a firm corrective jerk and walk the other way. Praise the dog after each and every correction. Maintain a good relationship with him so that he doesn't think he is being punished. Test the dog's level of training by placing him in "Sit-Stay." Open the door and see if he'll remain in position. At no time should you let go of the leash. Once the dog is responding well you can then answer the door yourself as the dog walks with you. Place him in "Sit-Stay" before opening the door and chances are he will no longer run out.

TAKING FOOD FROM THE TABLE

Stealing food from a set table or kitchen counter is not considered one of the more serious pet problems. As a matter of fact, almost every dog owner has at least one such favorite story about his little Princess. However, the habit is annoying and can cause considerable expense in view of the high cost of sirloin or prime rib.

This problem is somewhat similar to that of begging, which is covered elsewhere in this chapter. There are two things necessary to cure the dog of this bad habit. First, never feed the dog anything from the table or food-preparation area of the kitchen. Make this a hard-and-fast rule and do not allow anyone to violate it. This alone, after a while, will end the habit of expecting a reward for "hanging around." Next, bait him. After placing the leash and collar on him let him roam around as he pleases. Take a small quantity of freshly cooked food or food that you know appeals to him and leave it on a table or counter top. Step back and wait. When the dog goes for it, as he surely will, grab the leash and administer a hard corrective jerk accompanied by a loud "No." Immediately afterward praise him for obeying. Repeat this several times until he no longer tries to steal the food.

The use of the "throw can" is also very effective. For a young dog or puppy, yell "No" and shake the can vigorously. With an older dog, yell "No" and throw the can to the floor (do not hit him with the can). This type of correction will startle him and help to end the annoying habit.

TALKING BACK

One of the cutest things a dog can do is bark at you after you give him a command. It is especially true in the case of a puppy. People fall to the ground in laughter and many an owner actually regards it as though it were a terrific trick that he has taught the dog. The problem is that it is all too often an expression of defiance and unwillingness to respond to commands. Experience has proven that it leads to aggressiveness, where the dog, in some cases, becomes a bully. Usually, when a dog is given a command it is for a good reason and therefore should not be disobeyed, ignored, or protested. As undemocratic as it sounds, it is the only correct relationship between a dog and his master. The dog-owner relationship is pure feudalism. Dogs are totally dependent on their masters for everything connected with their well-being. And very often a command is very much in the best interests of the dog. Therefore, he must obey, and talking back is an indication of disobedience.

If your dog barks or howls at you after you give him a command he should be corrected. The corrective jerk with the leash and collar accompanied by a firm "No" will end this behavior. Don't forget to praise him immediately after the correction.

14 / Mature Problems Only

AFRAID OF CARS

Many dogs are afraid to ride in cars and run away the minute the car door is opened. Once forced inside, they generally whine, bark, or howl to be let out. Why? Perhaps they've had an unhappy experience with a car, or they feel trapped inside, or because it's simply a new and strange experience.

A car may have caused your dog to have a trauma you know nothing about. One of the great causes of dog deaths is heat prostration. It usually happens when an owner, ignorant of the small lung capacity of a dog, locks the animal in a car while shopping. Even on the mildest day with the windows rolled down a few inches the sun will immediately turn the car into an oven. The dog feels the intense heat and resulting oxygen shortage and panics when he finds that he can't get out. Eventually he will claw, scratch, and even hurl his body against the windows to get out. Often the result is death. But it is possible that the owner appears in the very early stages of this nightmare and, without knowing it, rescues the dog. After an experience like that it will be almost impossible to get the dog back into a car and the owner will never understand why. (Obviously, the windows of a car should always be open wide enough for good ventilation when locking a dog inside.) Heat prostration is only one of many traumas that a dog may have experienced while in a car by himself. Auto backfires, dogs in heat, teasing children, gasoline fumes, etc., are but a few of the possibilities.

Patience is the only solution. To begin with, make auto riding sound like fun. Turn it into a game. Get him in a cheerful mood with statements like, "Who wants a ride in the car? Let's go in the car, boy." Make it seem like a treat. If he won't take the bait then try coaxing him with a gentle tone of voice. Open the door on both sides and let him investigate on his own before starting up the engine. Once you get him inside on his own let him sniff around and leave if he wishes. Do not force him to stay. It is important that the dog never feels trapped with no way out. A cornered animal soon panics and behaves irrationally. Once he sits down, close the doors gently and start up. Drive one block and stop and let him out. If he gets back in then drive another block. If he refuses to get back into the car then let it go for another day. Try it again and again until the dog is relaxed enough to drive several miles. Petting him, praising him, and sitting in the back seat with him for a few minutes will also help to reassure him that nothing bad is going to happen. Do this three or four times a day for a few days and the problem will be solved.

CAR SICKNESS

There is really only one undeniable symptom of car sickness and that's when the dog loses control of his orifices and either vomits, urinates, or defecates all over the seat. Certainly, one possible reason for car sickness is feeding and watering before a long trip. With stop-and-go traffic the dog gets nauseous and loses control one way or another. A good rule is never feed or water a dog immediately before taking him in an automobile. And don't let the dog get overexcited before a trip. His running around will sometimes lead to the unpleasant physical sensations that cause car sickness.

If a dog is not really relaxed about riding in a car, he is going to have intense emotions that will induce car sickness. Therefore, it would be desirable to allow him to slowly adjust to riding in gradual stages. Open the door to the car and allow him to walk in by his own choice. Let him smell around and walk outside the other door if he wishes. Let him sit in the car for a few minutes without actually starting the engine. Let him claim the car as part of his territory before driving off. Animals panic if they feel trapped in an unfamiliar situation. When you finally decide to give him his first ride, have him sit in the back seat and hold on to his leash from the front seat. Drive a block and stop. Get out for a minute or two and then try it again. Repeat this process until you feel the dog is relaxed enough to continue without stopping.

It is also useful to convince the dog that riding in a car is fun. Try relating to the dog with cheerful enthusiasm just before entering the car. "Want to go for a ride? Come on, boy.

Let's get in the car." This kind of entreaty does work in changing the dog's attitude about riding. If the dog is not emotionally upset, then chances are he will not get car sick.

On the other hand, you do not want him to be uncontrollable. Maintain a firm control of the leash so that he does not jump around. Give him the command "Sit" and correct him if he does something wrong. The commands "Down" and "Stay" before driving off will undoubtedly help. The idea is to get him to ride in the back quietly and be a good passenger. Sometimes opening the window three or four inches is enough to satisfy him. It makes him feel less trapped and allows him to enjoy the fresh air and scenery. However, it is not a good idea to allow him to keep his head outside the window while the car is in motion. It can create eye irritations.

CHASING CARS

When a dog chases after a car he creates a clear and present danger, not only to his own life but to the occupants of the car he is chasing. It is horrible enough to think about him getting under the wheels of the moving vehicle, but what if the car smashes into a pole or tree in an effort to avoid the offending animal? There have been situations where a driver was startled and was made victim of a head-on collision with another car. For these reasons car chasing must be taken very seriously.

There are many possible reasons for a dog behaving this way in the face of terrible danger. One explanation is the instinct of the dog to be a running hunter. In his wild state, the dog (or wolf) must outrun his prey if he is to eat. This instinct is clearly demonstrated in greyhound racing where a mechanical rabbit is used as bait. Another possible explanation is that the dog might have had a bad experience with a moving car, i.e., backfire, a near-miss by a passing vehicle, or something tossed at him from a car window. Motor noises, exhaust fumes, or any number of factors may have conspired to create this abnormal reaction to moving autos. It is one of those rare situations where a knowledge of the cause offers little help in ending the problem.

What is needed here is to communicate to the dog that chasing cars displeases you and offers nothing but intense discomfort for his efforts. A strong choke collar and training leash can be employed the next time the dog indulges his habit. Let him go to the end of his leash as he runs toward the moving vehicle. Then pull for all you're worth, yanking him off his feet. As he reaches the end of the leash shout "No." Then praise him. If the problem does not end, then use a long length of rope in the same manner. Make sure it is a double thickness of strong rope so that he doesn't break it when he reaches the end. The longer the distance, the harder the impact when he reaches the end of it. You cannot allow yourself to be squeamish and hold back on that hard yank. It is absolutely certain that it will give the dog a great discomfort. But compare that very temporary discomfort with getting entangled in the wheels of a moving car.

THE SENSUOUS DOG—MOUNTING, ETC.

Mature female dogs go into heat twice a year for a two-week period and have very little, if any, interest in sex at other times. However, mature male dogs can become sexually aroused at any time, depending on their degree of sexual frustration and pent-up energy. If the mature male has never been mated and has little opportunity for his daily exercise requirement, then chances are he will mount the leg of a child or adult whenever aroused. If he is constantly segregated from female dogs, he will probably develop strong human attachments which can, at times, be sexual in nature. The habit of mounting is more than just embarrassing. If a large dog attempts to mount a young child he can inflict mental and physical injury. It is, however, not a common occurrence. Most mounting problems consist of a sexually frustrated dog wrapping around the leg of his owner or friend and simulating the movements of coitus.

Any mounting behavior should be dealt with immediately. Mating the male dog is one answer. Another is to give him plenty of daily exercise and allow him to work off the sexual energy. It does help. But, finally, when all else fails the dog must be corrected. Put his choke collar and leash on him and wait for him to mount. The minute he tries it, administer a hard corrective jerk and say "No" in a firm voice. Make the correction a tough one and do not allow the dog to get very far before administering it. If the dog is allowed to get very intense in this activity he may snap when you try to stop him.

It is best to stop him as quickly as possible. A loud shaking of the "throw can" may be used effectively as an alternative to the corrective jerk. And this is one of the few circumstances where we recommend raising the knee to the dog's chest to knock him down. No matter which technique you use it should be made very clear, as soon as possible, that mounting humans is totally unacceptable behavior.

SNIFFING UNDER DRESSES

Without being too graphic, it is quite clear that this is an embarrassing, annoying, and definitely undesirable problem. It is hardly necessary to deal with why a dog develops the habit. What is important is that he be broken of it.

Once again use the choke collar and leash. When the dog begins to indulge his bad habit, grab the leash and execute a hard corrective jerk and a loud "No." If the dog is a small, fragile creature, shake the "throw can" vigorously and deliver a stern "No." It is important to communicate your displeasure strongly whenever the dog misbehaves.

15/ Problem Dogs

The following problems occur after the dog has matured completely. They are so difficult to solve that the aid of a professional trainer is suggested. What can be done to help is to clarify the problems. This will allow you to recognize them so that you do not aggravate the situation, thus making them more difficult to solve.

BITING

A biter is a dog who has been *allowed* to become a biter. It could be a result of the growling that was never dealt with or the overaggressiveness that was never stopped. If you hit a dog enough times he is going to bite you. With the exception of dogs with congenital damage, no puppy was ever born with a vicious desire to bite. Why does a dog who licked your face when he was seven weeks old become a biter or even a killer at one or two years old? Usually because he has been hit during the housebreaking period, has had his nose rubbed in his own mess, has been kicked, has had objects thrown at him or fingers pointed at him, or has been swacked with rolled newspapers. If punishment has been the keynote every day of the dog's life, as it has been for some dogs, then he probably is the terror of the neighborhood. The dog has been trapped and his only way out has been to bite—usually the hands that feed him. If you hit with your hands he's going to bite at your hands.

It is sometimes dangerous to give a corrective jerk to this type of dog. He may react by biting you. He will bite especially if he knows he can get away with it. There is little the average owner can do other than restrain the dog at all times and seek the services of a professional trainer. If you don't, then we suggest you take out a large personal liability insurance policy.

FEAR BITING

The fear biter is different from the usual biter. The biter is an aggressive dog who is not afraid of anything. The fear biter is just the opposite, even though he has been abused just like the aggressive dog. He has experienced all the punishments and assaults that the other one has, but he has reacted conversely. He is afraid. He bites out of fear. If you confront a fear biter, he will back away until you turn around, at which point he will bite you on the calf, the rump, the hand, or the arm. A fear biter is extremely aggressive when on-leash, but cowers when released and runs away. His bravado comes from the security of being with his master and he will bark menacingly when a stranger comes into the house. If you yell at him or confront him in any way he runs. The minute you turn your back on him he will nail you. This kind of dog also bites if he is cornered under a table or chair. If he feels trapped and has no escape he will become aggressive.

His problems could have been caused by a combination of factors such as poor breeding and harsh treatment as a puppy and young dog. Again, there is little an owner can do without expert assistance. Training techniques for these various problems are complex and difficult and require a skilled handler.

GROWLING

A growl is a menacing sound that comes from deep in the throat of a dog and should be taken as a warning to stop what you are doing or to come no closer. In most cases this warning should not be taken lightly. Growling very often is the result of hitting the dog when he was young or delivering excessive or abusive corrections. Using the hands for punishment (hitting, slapping, pointing, etc.) helps to create a growler.

Growling can be the beginning of a dog turning on his master. It is important to understand that dogs never turn on their masters unless they have been abused in some way, and this applies to Dobermans and Shepherds. All too often you never know the other side of the story when you hear about a Doberman who turned on his master and attacked him. A puppy comes into the house and the owners, in their ignorance or frustration, slap the dog for every false move. After ten or twelve weeks of being hit, a conditioned reflex is created in the dog's brain and he flinches at every sudden movement. The dog grows up in fear and finally starts to fight back.

If a dog has grown up thinking of the human hand as an instrument of punishment, he will growl the minute a hand is used for anything to do with him. Some dogs will growl if you try to take something from their mouths or if you try to pet them.

Growling is also the result of spoiling the dog and never correcting him (in the proper way, of course) for anything. If he is allowed to get away with all manner of bad behavior, he is likely to growl when he finally is disciplined. From his perspective his owner is turning on him, so he growls in anger or defense. If his behavior is effective in getting things his way, he continues until he becomes a bully.

If the dog were still a puppy he could be taught with a firm corrective jerk and a stern "No." It is not so simple with a fully grown dog, however. It is important to understand why the dog is growling. If it's caused by you for any reason, punishment will only make matters worse. As a matter of fact, you will probably get bitten. If this problem has gone on for a year or two and you are terrorized by the dog, you have only two alternatives: call a professional trainer . . . or get rid of the dog.

DOG FIGHTING

Fighting usually happens between male dogs. It is sometimes so unpleasant that the joys of owning a dog are completely obscured. For those who own dogs in the city it is especially trying due to the large dog population. You find yourself avoiding the dog's walk or avoiding his romp in the park, for fear of meeting up with another dog and witnessing another fight. Your dog may have started fighting because he was attacked by another dog when he was very small. If so he will never like other male dogs. The best you can hope to do is control him when he is around other dogs. Another source of the problem from puppyhood is if he was allowed to attack a larger dog in play. The larger dog may tolerate his impish behavior and everyone may think it's cute, but if he becomes accustomed to challenging another dog he soon will be doing so on a permanent basis.

If your dog does get into a fight, there are a couple of ways to stop it. (However, never place your hand near the dog's face. In the heat of battle a dog doesn't know whom he's biting.) If the dog is on-leash, turn around and walk the other way, giving the dog a very hard pull. If the dog is not a Toy or not too big, pick him up off the ground by the leash. If he is choking he cannot do much of anything. If the dog is off the leash pull him up by the tail. Again, do this if the dog is not too big. If he is a short-tailed dog pick him up by his back legs. Use the corrective jerk as effectively as you can. Maintain the collar high on the dog's neck so that he will feel the full impact of the jerk. When he is about to engage in a fight with another dog give him a very hard corrective jerk. When the collar is low on his neck he hardly feels the tug of a correction. When all else fails, seek the services of a professional trainer.

THE NERVOUS DOG

The nervous dog reacts to ordinary situations differently from the average dog. If he gets excited he will wet. He is afraid of traffic, afraid of going outdoors, afraid of strangers, and afraid of other dogs. These high-strung dogs are very often the result of poor commercial breeding. But there are environmental situations that could also have caused such abnormal behavior. For example, if the dog has had several owners and was commanded in different ways each time, he may have developed a nervous temperament. The confusion leads to insecurity and an inability to please the current master. The result is a nervous dog. Very often the dog will acquire the inconsistent tendencies of his owner. Sometimes a nervous or neurotic dog reflects a nervous or neurotic master. Dogs are sometimes made nervous from traumatic experiences such as being too close to an auto backfire or a gunshot. If a dog was not taken outside the house for the first six months of his life a bad first experience could severely frighten him. Pampering the dog and making him overly dependent upon the owner can make him run away at the sight of a stranger. The problem is prevalent among the Toy breeds. The minute they leave the protection of the human "mother" they get the shakes, start to whine, and wet on the floor. Sometimes dogs resent the introduction of children into "their" house and become nervous. A totally dependent dog gets upset and nervous when a new child intrudes into the routine of the dog's life.

There is no fun in owning a nervous dog. Much of the pleasure that one usually has with a dog is completely missing. Some of these nervous problems can be solved if the dog is treated like a dog rather than a human child. It does not necessarily mean less attention, but a different kind of attention. Let the dog go out for frequent walks and meet other dogs. Do not hold him too much as if he were an infant. In general, do not use the dog as a substitute for a baby. In most cases of nervous dogs one should see a professional trainer.

OVERAGGRESSIVENESS

An overaggressive dog is not merely an exuberant or playful animal. His behavior is characterized by his ability to demonstrate to children, adults, or other dogs that he does not like them. The overaggressive dog will lunge, chase, push, growl, bark, dog-fight, or even bite to prove his point. Any negative, abnormal behavior falls into this category. It does no good to indulge in rationalizations about it. To say that the dog is perfectly behaved except if you get too close, or any other excuse like that, is to leave yourself open to much trouble.

If the dog were still a puppy any of the above-mentioned traits could be eliminated with a corrective jerk and a firm "No." If the dog was not corrected for this symptomatic behavior as a puppy then the result is an aggressive dog and that is not easy to cure. There are many reasons for abnormal behavior, both known and unknown, and the average dog owner is simply not equipped to deal with the problem. Sometimes a change of environmental conditions offers the best cure. But one must understand the nature of the dog's specific problem to make the proper change. Professional help must be sought.

THE SHY DOG

A shy dog is a variation of the nervous dog. Again, it can be due to poor commercial breeding. Or he may have been the runt of the litter and was bullied by the others. It is often unknown factors that create the shy dog. But no matter what the reason, he should be handled with *tender loving care.* If the dog is frightened of most things it will take a great deal of patience to cope with him. Few demands should be made on the dog and he should be showered with love and affection. Many dogs with this problem have responded to love and kindness. The problem must be coped with because shyness leads to nervousness which can turn the dog into a fear biter. Consult a professional trainer.

PART III

The Breeds

A Dictionary of Training

If you have recently purchased a dog, or if you are *about* to purchase a dog, this section will be of considerable help. Here, the training problems unique to the specific breeds are explored. It is obvious that a German Shepherd will pose a different set of problems from a Toy Poodle. It is exactly those differences that are dealt with in this portion of the book.

This part is divided into the six breed groupings as defined by the American Kennel Club. They are: Sporting Dogs, Hounds, Working Dogs, Terriers, Toys, and Non-sporting Dogs. Within these groupings, each breed is listed alphabetically and is dealt with as extensively as possible. Part III of *Good Dog, Bad Dog* is a dictionary of training problems indicative of the sixty-six breeds that are listed.

Each breed is discussed in terms of its Positive Characteristics, Negative Characteristics, and Specific Training Problems as a mature animal. It is a fair assumption that all puppy problems and solutions apply to every breed. This information will offer some aid in knowing what to expect from the dog of your choice. It is important to understand why you prefer one breed over another. Some people want a dog for protection. Others want a family pet, a gift for children or an elderly couple, relief from loneliness, or a friend and companion. To anyone shopping for an animal, it is suggested that he familiarize himself with the many breeds available. Each breed fulfills many combinations of needs. To know about each breed and understand what you personally want from a dog helps you make the correct choice. For those who have already brought a dog into their homes, this section will give them a clear idea of what to expect from it.

The following dictionary of training is based on information learned the hard way. It represents a synthesis of the first-hand experience that coauthor Matthew Margolis has gained in his capacity as owner-operator of the National Institute of Dog Training, Inc. He has trained well over five thousand dogs representing every breed listed in this section. Where a breed has been omitted, it is simply because he has had too little experience with it. The dogs he has trained have come from every conceivable source. Many have been among the most expensive dogs from the most exclusive kennels. Others have come from pet shops, adoption agencies, the ASPCA, private kennels, commercial kennels, and even home litters.

It stands to reason that not all specimens of each breed will be alike. But when training hundreds of dogs from any one particular breed, certain behavioral patterns become apparent. These patterns formulate the basis for Mr. Margolis's evaluations.

While not attempting to upgrade one breed at the expense of another, it is all too clear that some breeds are more responsive to training than others; some are more willing to please; some are more independent. Mr. Margolis has attempted to give a fair appraisal of each dog's temperament. It is all based on his personal experience and may contradict the legitimate experiences of any number of individual dog owners. But it is asked that one consider the source of the dog. A specific dog may come from a superior bloodline, and that certainly would be a factor in any contradiction. The converse of this also holds true. Some dogs are the poor result of too much inbreeding, even though they are of a well-tempered breed. The appraisals offered here have been determined by experience with a cross-section of dogs from each breed. It is felt that this part can help the prospective dog owner anticipate what to expect from the breed of his choice.

Dogs differ in personality and behavior as do people. For every person there is a dog to match his personality, needs, and desires. What is a negative factor for one person could very well be a positive factor for another. Do not turn a jaundiced eye on a breed that has a long list of negative characteristics. Those traits that are considered negative may be the very traits that would endear the dog to you and thus afford fifteen years of pleasure and gratification. All dogs are good guys until proven otherwise.

Group I

Sporting Dogs

POINTER, GERMAN SHORTHAIRED

Positive characteristics. Members of this breed are very lovable and capable of giving great warmth and affection. They are friendly and exceptionally good with children. Powerful dogs such as these are very good in the country because they have a great desire to run and need a great deal of exercise. If they are kept in the country and get the proper amount of exercise they will be very responsive to training. They make excellent companions.

bined with an accumulation of pent-up energy, results in total

Negative characteristics. German Shorthaired Pointers are very high-strung animals. They are nervous, excitable dogs. Unless they are given sufficient daily exercise, it is difficult to keep them in an apartment. Their desire to jump, com-

chaos. They will jump on furniture, jump on people, steal food from the table, get into the garbage, and chew anything, whether it's nailed down or not.

These are stubborn dogs with very strong wills. If the owner is not very firm, his animal will be a constant source of trouble. These dogs require a great deal of authority. If the owner spoils the dog he will regret it for the rest of the dog's life. These Pointers must be trained as soon as possible. If the owner waits the customary year to begin training it may be too late. Strict training should begin after the third month.

Specific training problems. Use a good strong choke collar and a six-foot leash. When executing a corrective jerk be certain the leash does not get caught in the dog's long, flapping ears. It can cause him great pain and make him aggressive.

Because these are hunting dogs, they are not as attentive as other breeds. They are constantly indulging their keen senses of smell and must be forced to pay attention to commands. After the dog obeys a command, wait four seconds to give him praise, and do not be too exuberant. In the "Heel," try to keep their attention by talking to them. The more you capture their attention the more responsive they will be.

These dogs should be worked exceptionally hard in the "Stay," since they are not too good at it and will remain in "Stay" for only a short time. It is especially important in the city where there are so many distractions to lead them into trouble or danger.

They should never be allowed off-leash in the city. Their greatest difficulty is in the command "Come When Called."

Because these are hunting dogs, they must be made to obey absolutely. The more obedience training they are given the more responsive they will be in the city. One of the best ways to keep them out of mischief indoors is to give them a place that is exclusively their own in the apartment or house. (See Chapter 12, "Go to Your Place.")

Hunting dogs must be obedience-trained more vigorously than other breeds if they are going to share a house or an apartment with a family. Vigorous obedience training at an early age is the key to enjoying the many pleasant aspects of this breed.

RETRIEVER, GOLDEN

Positive characteristics. Golden Retrievers are a very friendly breed. They are considered by many to be the most ideal pets because of their lovable behavior. They are affectionate, warm, and very good with children. These dogs have few grooming requirements and are good in either apartment or house. As a breed they are extremely responsive to training and execute commands with great ease. For this reason they are used frequently as Seeing Eye Dogs.

Negative characteristics. Because they are hunting dogs, their minds stray from time to time, making them inattentive. Occasionally they are nervous, but this can be caused by inbreeding. It is not true of the entire breed. If possible, the prospective owner should examine the dam and the sire for nervousness.

Although these are not stubborn dogs, they do take advantage of the owner when they can. They must be told what to do and made to obey each command.

Specific training problems. When you execute a corrective jerk, be certain that the leash does not get caught in the dog's long, flapping ears. It can cause him great pain and make him aggressive.

After the dog obeys a command, wait two seconds to give him praise and do not be too exuberant. In almost all the basic commands Golden Retrievers have a tendency to inch up after obeying. That is an infraction of the rules, and if they are allowed to get away with it they will become less and less responsive. When giving the "Sit" make sure they "Stay" for a short period of time without moving. When executing the "Heel" do not let them walk ahead. The same applies to the "Down" and the "Down-Stay." "Come When Called" may be a problem in the city. Remember, they are hunters. Do not give this command in the city without a leash. It is dangerous.

One of the best ways to keep these dogs out of mischief is to give them a place that is exclusively their own in the apartment or house. (See Chapter 12, "Go to Your Place.")

Hunting breeds are not usually considered city dogs. However, because of their beauty and many other attributes they are desired by many urban dwellers. It is therefore recommended in that case that an intense training program be initiated as soon as possible.

RETRIEVER, LABRADOR

Positive characteristics. Because of their keen hunting instincts, these dogs are generally considered better for the country. They adjust perfectly to family life and are very tolerant and patient with children. Labradors are being used more and more as Seeing Eye Dogs for the blind, and that speaks highly of their ability to be trained. That ability is good for all types of training, including basic obedience and guard work. Because they respond to human beings so well, they can be taught much more readily than many other breeds.

They are one of the most intelligent of the breeds and enjoy a long life span.

Negative characteristics. Dogs of this breed require a great deal of exercise, which can be a problem for the ones who live in apartments. They would have to be exercised at least two or three times a week to make up for the lack of country life. Like all hunting breeds, Labradors are not ideal for the elderly. They are too energetic and physically demanding and they require a firm, strong hand.

Specific training problems. When executing the corrective jerk, be certain the leash does not get caught in the dog's long, flapping ears. It can cause him great pain and make him aggressive.

Be certain your dog obeys all commands the first time with no delays, otherwise he will take advantage of you and only obey when he feels like it. Make great demands of the dog and enforce all commands. Give immediate praise after a command is obeyed. Be exuberant. Do not allow him off-leash in the city.

Obedience training must be initiated in puppyhood to avoid the characteristic mischief a Labrador Retriever can create in an apartment situation.

Labrador Retrievers are usually not aggressive. However, many become that way after being hit by their owners with either a hand or a rolled-up newspaper. The most good-natured dog has his turning point and will only take so much hitting. This breed is one of the most tolerant and your Labrador will remain so if he is not physically abused. One of the best ways to keep him out of mischief is to give him a place that is exclusively his own in the apartment or house. (See Chapter 12, "Go to Your Place.")

SETTER, ENGLISH

Positive characteristics. English Setters are easygoing to the point of lethargy. Unlike most other hunting breeds, they are ideally suited to elderly people because of their sedate temperaments. They adjust to apartment life very well. These dogs are wonderful with children. In fact they are so gentle they will let you do almost anything to them without ever complaining or acting aggressive.

Negative characteristics. They are very stubborn, strong-willed, and difficult to housebreak. And they can develop destructive chewing problems if left alone. But their stubbornness takes the form of resistance rather than uncontrollable obstinacy. Instead of pulling on a leash, they simply will not walk. Instead of going into "Sit," they will lie down. When called they will come slowly instead of the immediate response that a command demands.

Specific training problems. The basic obedience commands must be handled with great diligence, more so than with other breeds. Extra patience is required and also extra firmness. After a command is obeyed, give immediate praise and be very exuberant.

Setters must be made to obey each command. For example, if your dog refuses to "Heel," you might go so far as to get on the ground and call him to you, backing up a little as he comes, all the while praising him and giving him confidence. This gets the dog moving but at the same time gives him the opportunity to feel at ease about it. Strongarm tactics with this breed will bring nothing but disappointment.

The "Down" and "Down-Stay" will be very difficult to teach. The dog will fight you every inch of the way. In this case the training sessions should be broken up into shorter sessions and spread over a longer period of time.

They do not respond quickly to "Come When Called." With most Setters a slow response is to be expected. These dogs will rebel at browbeating. Therefore, they should be trained as puppies while they are still carefree, playful, and energetic. One of the best ways to keep them out of mischief is to give them a place that is exclusively their own in the apartment or house. (See Chapter 12, "Go to Your Place.")

There are many years of rewarding pleasure ahead if the city dweller begins an obedience program when this member of the hunting breeds is a puppy.

SETTER, GORDON

Positive characteristics. These gentle, friendly dogs are very good with children. Their need to run and exercise in open spaces makes them ideal country dogs. For the connoisseur or fancier, they are special, uncommon, stylish, almost regal-looking. This intelligent breed, with its handsome black and tan coat, has the bearing of strength and great dignity.

Negative characteristics. Gordon Setters are stubborn. One of the reasons they are not seen in the city very often is the difficulty they have adjusting to apartment life. Although they are not the largest breed, they behave as though they were and require a firm, strong hand from their masters.

Specific training problems. Exercise care in administering the corrective jerk. Their long ears can get caught in the choke collar and leash.

Housebreaking should begin immediately. Gordon Setters, like most other hunting breeds, have a hard time with house-breaking. Paper training should never be started and then abandoned for housebreaking. It is difficult for them to un-learn one thing and adjust to something new.

In administering corrections, the first jerk should be quite firm rather than wasting five or six easy jerks. The more you jerk the more they will rebel. One hard jerk will be enough to let them know who's boss. Give immediate praise after a command is obeyed and be very exuberant.

Do not let them off-leash in the city. Like other hunting dogs they become distracted with squirrels, pigeons, and other animals and refuse to "Come When Called." Their response to this command is unreliable even with a leash.

In an apartment, Gordons manifest many annoying prob-lems such as chewing, jumping on furniture, going into gar-bage, etc., which is precisely why an early start with obedi-ence training is important. Problems that arise in puppyhood are difficult to end as the dog matures. It is important to men-tion that this breed should never be fed from the table. Once you start you will have a canine dinner guest for the rest of his life and he can be a large nuisance. One of the best ways to keep him out of mischief is to give him a place that is exclu-sively his own in the apartment or house. (See Chapter 12, "Go to Your Place.")

If the Gordon Setter is to be enjoyed as a pet rather than as the hunter he was meant to be, then it is definitely advisable to begin obedience training at an early age. Three months old is not too soon.

SETTER, IRISH

Postive characteristics. Temperamentally, these dogs are affectionate and loving, gentle and sweet-natured. Excellent hunters, they are ideal country residents. Irish Setters are easy to groom, have good appetites, and adjust to family life very well.

Negative characteristics. They are very stubborn dogs. Their strong wills require firmness in all training matters. It is important to administer strong corrections when they ignore commands, otherwise they tend to do as they please. Obviously, they are not convenient for elderly people. Training must begin as early as possible to avoid adult problems that begin in puppyhood. If these dogs are not trained properly they can literally ruin an apartment. It starts with messing in the middle of a good carpet and ends with chewing expensive furniture to sawdust. However, they can adjust to apartment life if given an obedience course from the minute they first enter the household.

Specific training problems. Irish Setters have extremely long ears which can get caught in the leash and choke collar when a corrective jerk is administered. So be cautious. Wait three or four seconds after the dog obeys a command to give him praise and do not be too exuberant.

Setters have difficulty with housebreaking. This part of their training will not be easy. Every aspect outlined in the housebreaking chapter should be applied with diligence, i.e., diet, walks, etc. They must be watched carefully until the housebreaking is completed.

The correction "No" does not work effectively unless they have come to associate it with a firm corrective jerk. Throughout most of the training period the corrective jerk should be administered firmly but not excessively. Too many corrections will make the dog jerk shy. Next to housebreaking, walking in "Heel" is their biggest problem. One minute they will walk in perfect "Heel" and the next minute jerk your arm out running to play with another dog. They are very easily distracted and use force to get what they want. It is important that heeling be strictly enforced. Never allow one infraction of this rule without administering a corrective jerk.

Never allow this breed off-leash in the city. Irish Setters have been known to run off and never return. City life imposes a limitation on much-needed exercise and creates a great deal of pent-up energy that can be destructive. For this reason alone these dogs should not be allowed off-leash in the city. One of the best ways to keep them out of mischief indoors is to give them a place that is exclusively their own in the apartment or house (See Chapter 12, "Go to Your Place.")

SPANIEL, COCKER

Positive characteristics. Cocker Spaniels are sturdy animals, capable of taking strong correction. If trained at an early age, they will respond quickly to any command they have been taught. They will "Heel" perfectly and lie down on command almost the instant it is given. They are excellent with children and adapt to apartment life very well. Because they are not very large dogs they do not require too much exercise. Because they are not too active or rambunctious they can be handled easily by elderly people. They are ideal for people who want an in-between dog.

Negative characteristics. Due to excessive inbreeding many Cocker Spaniels have become aggressive. In addition, if they are hit they will become growlers, biters, dog fighters, and generally hostile. It is not because of the breed but rather the inbreeding. Spaniels have appeared in recorded English history as far back as the twelfth century and have developed a large popularity in the United States. The Cocker Spaniel is a subdivision of the land Spaniel and is identified as the smaller of the Spaniels, which accounts for its great popularity in this country. It is this popularity that has led to its massive inbreeding, much to the detriment of the breed. The best advice is to exercise caution and selectivity before purchasing one. Investigate the puppy's pedigree. If possible, examine his parents; ask a lot of questions. Try to evaluate the temperament of his progenitors. You should do all this because only a well-bred specimen will respond favorably to training.

Specific training problems. Cocker Spaniels are hunters and have the same problems as the other hunting breeds. Avoid entangling their long ears in the choke collar and leash when administering the corrective jerk.

These mischievous dogs will jump on furniture, take food from the table, jump on people, etc. These are problems that must be solved in puppyhood or they will remain throughout the life of the dog. If you allow the puppy to sit on your lap he will eventually jump up on people. If you let him sleep on the bed he will jump on the furniture.

When giving Cocker Spaniels commands, make sure they are forced to respond. If you give in at the beginning they can never be relied upon to obey. Wait two seconds after the dog obeys a command to give him praise, and be exuberant. "Go to Your Place" is very useful for Cockers because they tend to get into mischief, and this will give you a tool for control. "Down-Stay" is useful, too. "Down-Stay" will also help in the car. They don't travel well as a rule. Excitement or nervousness makes them jump from seat to seat; "Down-Stay" makes them stop.

Hitting this breed can cause more behavioral damage than with other breeds. The result will be a nasty animal. Housebreaking is usually when hitting begins, and with Cocker Spaniels that's the beginning of an aggressive temperament. Most of the negative characteristics can be avoided if you exercise self-control and avoid hitting or terrorizing the dog in any way.

Cocker Spaniels are hunters and as such are best in the kennel of an estate. However, if yours is a house pet he must be obedience-trained as a puppy so that you may both enjoy fifteen years of pleasant relations.

SPANIEL, ENGLISH SPRINGER

Positive characteristics. Springer Spaniels are good city dogs and good country dogs. They make excellent pets for children and elderly people. They adjust well to apartment life, are easy to get along with, are well suited to training, and adapt easily to most situations. Beauty and utility are combined in this even-tempered breed.

Negative characteristics. Recently Springer Spaniels have developed medical problems such as eczema and general skin irritations. A close scrutiny of the individual dog's bloodlines should be made before purchase.

Specific training problems. Like all hunting dogs, they are difficult to housebreak. Housebreaking should begin as soon as possible.

Be careful of the dog's long ears when administering the corrective jerk. Do not catch them in the choke collar and leash. Give immediate praise after a command is obeyed and be exuberant.

During all training, but specifically the "Heel," be alert to their tendency to wander away and become distracted by other animals, as is characteristic of all hunting dogs. If you bear down on the "Heel," you will not have problems with the other commands. "Go to Your Place" is important for this breed. "Down-Stay" is another important command. These commands give you tools for greater control and make it easier for the dog to please you.

Vigorous obedience training at an early age is the key to enjoying the many pleasant aspects of this breed.

VIZSLA

Positive characteristics. These natives of Hungary are very good with children. They make wonderful house pets and are also good in the country. They adapt very well to apartment life. Appetite is never a problem (except during illness) and their life span is from twelve to fifteen years. This short-coated breed requires very little grooming. Because of their short coats they do not shed very much. Sweet-natured and affectionate, the Vizsla is well suited to training and responds without too much correction.

Negative characteristics. Like other hunting breeds, they are stubborn. Occasionally, due to poor breeding, they develop a problem of nervous wetting. Inbreeding has created many nervous Vizslas. Although they are good apartment dogs, there is one qualification. If training does not begin at a very young age they develop chewing problems and cause much destruction. Even a trained Vizsla will chew up an apartment if he is not exercised regularly. Chewing is caused by confinement. Exercise combined with obedience training is the only answer.

Specific training problems. Administering the corrective jerk is critical with this breed. Their ears are very long and get tangled in the choke collar and leash, which can be very painful for the animal. Be careful. Wait four seconds after the dog obeys a command to give him praise and do not be too exuberant.

Vizslas are difficult to housebreak. Never paper train them if you plan to switch to housebreaking later on. The changeover is almost impossible for them. Do not correct a puppy if he fails to use the paper when messing indoors. Simply confine him to one small area, as explained in the paper-training chapter.

These are very excitable animals and will cross in front of you or jump on you when learning to "Heel." Emphasize the "Heel" and do not let them pull you. They will respond to an authoritative voice. Because they crave affection in large doses, they will work very hard to please you. The trick is to know when to withhold the affection and when to give it as a reward for responding properly to a command.

With this breed emphasize the "Sit-Stay" and "Down-Stay." Vizslas tend to demand great attention from anyone who enters the house. They also like to run out the door the minute it is opened. By emphasizing the "Stay" command, you will be able to maintain a greater control over them. "Go to Your Place" is another important command.

The plains of Hungary are the natural habitat of this great hunting breed. Keeping one as a house pet demands that obedience training begin at a very early age if the dog is to live compatibly in a domestic situation.

WEIMARANER

Positive characteristics. There is a great ambivalence in most Weimaraner owners. They are stubbornly loyal and absolutely devoted to these "Gray Ghosts," despite the many difficulties involved in owning one.

Weimaraners are excellent companions for children. They have a tremendous tolerance for the rough-and-tumble treatment usually meted out by small children. They will endure a child's eye-gouging, ear-pulling, back-sitting, and tail-yanking. Because of their need for exercise, they will run a great deal and can be a joy to behold in the country. The more exercise they get the better they are to live with.

These German hunting dogs are strong and lively and can be used effectively for guard work. They can be trained to growl, bark, or bite on command. Protective of their families by nature, they adapt to this work very well. However, guard work can only be accomplished with expert training. Because of their even temperament, they can be trained to bite one minute and lick the victim's face the next. A short-coated breed, they require very little grooming and do not shed.

Negative characteristics. Weimaraners embody all the negative characteristics of the hunting breeds. They are stubborn and self-willed and try to get away with everything possible. At times they do not obey commands. They will wander off if given the chance. If their pent-up energy is not released in some positive form of exercise, they are capable of destroying entire apartments.

Once they understand that the master does not operate with great authority, they will take large liberties such as pulling him down the street. Such liberties are usually taken with women owners. Because Weimaraners are so lovable, women find it hard to avoid mothering them.

Weimaraners are dog fighters. They are not recommended for elderly people. They require a firm, strong hand and will respond to nothing else. Chewing problems are common in this breed. They are notorious for destroying, in some instances, thousands of dollars' worth of furniture and personal posessions. Their chewing will try every ounce of patience you possess, and if one does not possess great patience it can be a difficult struggle to train them. It is a situation with built-in failure. Unless these dogs are forced to respond to obedience training through patience and authority, they will be miserable to own.

Specific training problems. Their long ears get tangled in the choke collar and leash. Be cautious when administering the corrective jerk. It is critical, because they require a very firm correction. Without firm correction they will take advantage of the owner and make a simple walk a living nightmare. They need to be handled with authority. These dogs will always test their owners to determine how much they can get away with. When administering a firm corrective jerk, do not be frightened if they whine and scream like babies. Even though you are stared at by strangers and thought to be murdering your dog, do not be fooled by this ploy. They are not hurt. Continue to deliver firm corrections, especially when teaching the "Heel." The "Sit-Stay" and "Down-Stay" will be very useful commands when control is needed, as it often is. Wait five seconds after the dog obeys a command to give him praise, and praise him in a subdued tone of voice.

They can be pests, demanding attention and affection when the situation does not call for it. That's when the "Stay" commands are very handy. Weimaraners should never be taken off-leash in the city. They are completely untrustworthy and will chase the first animal they see, which could cause a bad accident.

Like other hunting breeds, they are difficult to housebreak. They must be watched carefully. The housebreaking should begin as soon as possible. One of the best ways to keep members of this breed out of mischief is to give them a place that is exclusively their own in the apartment or house. (See Chapter 12, "Go to Your Place.")

Owners of this breed are legion in declaring their great pleasure and love in living with them. Weimaraners can be tolerable house pets only if they are trained at a very early age.

Group II

Hounds

AFGHAN HOUND

Positive characteristics. Many people consider these dogs beautiful in appearance and regal in manner. It is the quality of elegance that has made them so popular. There is great snob appeal connected with the Afghan. Their history is documented as far back as 3000 B.C., where they were seen on the Sinai Peninsula between Suez and Aqaba. Historically this breed has been identified with royalty, which would account for the ostentatious attitude of many Afghan owners. During the great days of the British Empire, Afghans were used for hunting the leopard. Despite their haughty, delicate look, they have been used for centuries as first-rate hunters in the mountainous regions of Afghanistan. In the United States these aristocratic hunters have been used primarily as ornamentation. If you enjoy fussing and primping, this is the breed for you. Their long, silken fur requires daily attention.

Negative characteristics. These are stubborn dogs and consequently offer much resistance to training. Although some *former* owners consider them stupid, it's not true. They merely lack a desire to please and manifest an unwillingness to learn. It is extremely hard to train them. Where most breeds can begin training after they reach twelve weeks, Afghans will not respond to training until they are at least six or seven months old. By that time, housebreaking becomes extremely difficult. Housebreaking should begin early. Many owners have experienced some degree of successful training.

The Afghan's tolerance for children is low and they are not ideally suited for apartment living. They can be aggressive bullies.

Specific training problems. Patience is absolutely essential. These dogs cannot be treated like any other breed. You must take your time throughout the training period. Give immediate praise after the dog obeys a command and be very exuberant.

Do not use a metal choke collar because it will ruin their silken fur. Either a leather or nylon choke collar is suggested. Do not work this breed for long periods, especially when teaching the "Heel" and the "Sit." Break up the training periods so there are more sessions for shorter periods of time.

Unless you are home a great deal and can walk them five or six times a day, you are going to have a terrible time housebreaking them. They must be caught in the act of messing indoors before they can be taught to understand what you expect.

Members of this breed do not want to be left alone. They can be very destructive and have been known to chew their way through large quantities of valuable furniture and personal possessions. Because of their stubbornness you will have to be extremely firm teaching the "Down" and "Down-Stay." Despite their great beauty and elegance, the training period will be a battle of wills between master and dog.

BASENJI

Positive characteristics. Basenjis are very well-tempered, loving, and affectionate animals. They are highly individualistic dogs who tend to attach themselves devotedly and loyally to one person. Adapting to city life very well, they make excellent apartment dogs. These are quiet dogs that never bark. Their short coats require very little grooming. They are responsive to training and indicate a willingness to please. Results are much greater if training begins at a young age. These enjoyable animals are distinguished by their almost human-looking faces. They are good with children and can take the rigors of a child's play. Because they are not a nervous breed, they can be left alone for many hours and still maintain their even temperaments.

Negative characteristics. Since they are stubborn dogs, we do not recommend them for elderly people. Once they decide to do something you will have to match their obstinacy with your firm authority every inch of the way. Because they are "barkless" they make poor guard dogs.

Specific training problems. Because of their stubbornness be sure to give each command properly. Be very firm and let them know who is boss. Give immediate praise after the dog obeys a command and be very exuberant. You should not have many training problems with this breed.

BASSET HOUND

Positive characteristics. Bassets are very good with children and make excellent house pets. Because they are not very active, they never run wild through the house. One could say there is an absence of overexcitement. Their lethargic demeanor joined with their droopy face are considered part of their charm. This breed has come into its own since advertising agencies discovered their amusing appeal and started making salesmen out of them on TV commercials. They are truly ideal apartment pets. They enjoy a normal life span (twelve to fifteen years) and have gentle, sweet temperaments. Bassets respond very well to training, even past the training period of the average dog.

Negative characteristics. They have very few negative traits. Housebreaking is sometimes a problem, but even that can be overcome if training begins early. Many Bassets are picky eaters.

Specific training problems. Pay attention to their long, floppy ears when administering the corrective jerk. They sometimes tangle in the choke collar and leash. It is very painful. In some cases the choke collar is not recommended. Whether or not to use it would be determined by the temperament of the dog.

In "Heel" your dog is going to have difficulty keeping up with you. Bassets walk much more slowly than other breeds and have trouble keeping up a brisk pace. It also takes them longer to go into the "Sit" than other breeds. You should make allowances. The "Stay" will be the easiest command for them. Maybe it's because they don't like getting up too often.

They respond more to praise and affection than correction. Give immediate praise when the dog obeys a command and be very exuberant. It is recommended that the corrective jerk be administered gently and not too often. You will get better results from a loving, gentle tone than from a firm discipline. The "Down" and "Come When Called" are good commands for them. These lovable animals are endearing and can make training sessions a delightful experience. Most professional trainers enjoy working with Basset Hounds.

BEAGLE

Positive characteristics. Beagles adjust well to apartment life or country life. These sweet little dogs look like stuffed toys and are very good with children. They are usually gentle, playful, and even tempered. They are hardy eaters with a good life span (twelve to fifteen years) and have a short coat that requires a minimum of grooming.

Negative characteristics. Because this is a stubborn breed, many owners try to use force to get their way. The consequences are many. Most important is that the dogs become aggressive and nasty if mistreated. They have been known to turn on their masters, bite children, growl, and get into dog fights. Much of this can be avoided if one exercises patience and a minimum of discipline. Force will only bring out the worst in them. The key to their training is to maintain an attitude of teaching as opposed to one of harsh discipline.

Specific training problems. Start training early to avoid the negative aspects described above. Even though they are stubborn, they are easy to teach at a young age. Watch their ears in administering the corrective jerk. A metal choke collar is not recommended if you are going to teach a puppy. Use nylon or leather. An older Beagle can tolerate a very fine metal choke collar.

Be firm but not harsh. Most of the basic commands will be relatively easy to teach. However, they offer resistance to the "Down." Give immediate praise when the dog obeys a command and be very exuberant.

When training these dogs, select a location that offers few,

if any, distractions. You must command their attention more
than the average breed.

BLACK AND TAN COONHOUND

Positive characteristics. Black and Tans are affectionate.
They enjoy the country much more than the city. They are
very responsive to training and have excellent appetites.

Negative characteristics. These dogs are not well suited to
city life. Like many of the hound breeds, they do not adapt
well to the restrictions of a small apartment. You must be
on top of them all the time. Their attention span in the city
is poor, owing to their inclination to wander, both mentally
and physically.

Specific training problems. As is true of many hounds, Black
and Tans abound in energy and require a great deal of exercise. There is nothing like a good long run to make them more
responsive to training. A good daily exercise program will
help them work off their nervous energy and make them
easier to live with in the city.

   Wait two seconds after the dog obeys a command to give
him praise, and do not be too exuberant.

BORZOI *(Russian Wolfhound)*

Positive characteristics. These are marvelous, elegant-looking
dogs. Thin and lanky, they move with great speed and dash.
Many city dwellers consider them status symbols and very
chic to own. Borzois are regal in stature and appeal to very
special types. In most instances, they are purchased for reasons of ornamentation or, perhaps, ostentation. These tall
beauties are easygoing, capable of sitting outside a fancy shop
for many hours, and staying put in the position in which they
were placed. Because they are not too active, they make excellent city pets. They are quiet, dignified animals who are
very willing to please. In their natural habitat Borzois are
hunters, and for that reason are very well suited to country
living like most of the sporting dogs.

Negative characteristics. Borzois are not especially suited to children. They do not respond well to rough treatment. Aloof animals, like cats, they neither ask for nor give much affection. People who own Borzois are often of the same temperament.

Specific training problems. One need not administer too many firm corrections. Give immediate praise when the dog obeys a command and be extremely exuberant. Giving them a great deal of praise whenever they respond properly will get better results than overcorrection.

Be gentle with the leash because they resist constant jerking. Show them what to do and they will do it.

DACHSHUND
(Smooth, Longhaired, Wirehaired)

Positive characteristics. These dogs are among the most even-tempered animals in existence. They are very good with children, and especially good with elderly people. Dachshunds, no matter what kind, are ideally suited to apartment living. Their eating habits are good and they live a long time. They require very little grooming. Very few people can resist their frisky, gentle manner.

Negative characteristics. Dachshunds are one of those breeds that have great difficulty making the transition from paper training to housebreaking. If you begin with paper training then you should stay with that technique. If, ultimately, you want the dog to go outside, then begin housebreaking from the start.

Specific training problems. Do not use any type of choke collar. Dachshunds have tender necks and can be hurt very easily, which is true of most small breeds. An ordinary leather collar will do the job.

If you begin training them as young as three months old, then work slowly. They need a lot of praise and affection. Wait one second after the dog obeys a command to give him praise and use an exuberant tone of voice. Do not use "No" too often. Small dogs can be frightened very easily, causing behavioral complications that are not inherent to their natures.

Exercise patience when teaching the "Sit." Because of the irregular shape of their bodies, it takes them longer to sit properly. They will be very slow getting into position. They also have trouble heeling properly. Their legs are very short, so they walk slower than the average dog. Consequently, they will not be able to keep up if you walk too quickly. You will probably have more problems with them lagging behind than pulling ahead.

Be patient reaching the "Stay" and the "Down." They are eager to please, but it takes them longer to respond to a new command than is usual with other dogs. They need a lot of praise. Dachshunds respond to "Come When Called" better than most commands, owing to their great desire for affection. Be sure to give them a lot of praise when they respond to this command.

GREYHOUND

Positive characteristics. It is the look and the elegance of the Greyhound that make them so appealing. Greyhound owners take great pleasure mentioning that this breed is the fastest in the world. Outside the racetrack they are not too common, which is another source of pride for the Greyhound owner. Their truly distinctive gait gives them an aristocratic air. They prance while they take their daily constitutional. That agility allows them to respond to commands very quickly. They adapt to country life best because there is an absence of noise and distraction. They are much more responsive when it's peaceful and quiet.

Negative characteristics. These timid, high-strung animals are not suitable for elderly people or children. They are a nervous breed and do not fare well in the city with its traffic noises, etc. Because of their high spirits, they do not make the ideal family dog. They are simply too nervous.

Specific training problems. Training should begin quite early in the dog's life. Gentleness is required. They cannot be jolted with too many firm corrections; they are too high strung for that. The best way to train this breed is to show them what to do and give them a good reason for doing it. They cannot take constant harassments such as "No," "Bad dog," and "Shame." Give immediate praise when the dog obeys a command and be exuberant. Do not expect the same kind of response that you would get from a German Shepherd or even a Beagle. They are highly excitable animals and require tender loving care.

IRISH WOLFHOUND

Positive characteristics. Rugged. playful, and protective, Irish Wolfhounds are very good with children and make ideal house pets. They are at their best in the country where they can run and play hard. It is difficult to resist their sweet, gentle natures and affectionate personalities. In the city they are lethargic for the most part and sleep a great deal, adjusting to apartment life quite easily. Their wiry coats require a minimum of grooming.

Negative characteristics. The very size of these dogs can discourage the city dweller from owning one. They are among the largest dogs in existence and require a great deal of food, so if economy is a consideration then you should think twice before buying one.

Specific training problems. Irish Wolfhounds require a very firm hand. Because they are so large, you cannot equivocate or back down from a command. If they get out of hand it could lead to serious problems. It would be impossible to handle a 34-inch, 175-pound Irish Wolfhound that suddenly became aggressive. That is why early training is absolutely necessary. Although this breed responds well to training, it does so at a slower pace than others. Irish Wolfhounds take a little longer to "Sit" and will lope to you on "Come When Called" rather than run swiftly.

If the dog is ever to be handled by a woman, it is essential that training take place while the dog is still small and manageable. Firmness is important. When using the corrective jerk, deliver it with great firmness. If you emphasize the "No" simultaneously, you will eventually be able to achieve the same corrective results without the jerk. The vocal correction will suffice.

Give immediate praise when the dog obeys a command and be exuberant.

NORWEGIAN ELKHOUND

Positive characteristics. Because they are inclined to bark a great deal, these animals are very good watchdogs. They love the roughhouse play of children and make excellent house pets in both city and country. They have good appetites, live between twelve and fifteen years, and are even tempered.

Negative characteristics. Norwegian Elkhounds shed profusely and must be brushed often to avoid clumps of fur on the furniture and floor. These excitable dogs run and play very hard and consequently are not recommended for elderly people. They are very stubborn and require a firm hand to control their tendency to take advantage of owners, especially those owners who allow them to get away with the slightest disobedience. If they are hit they will become aggressive.

Specific training problems. They respond very well to training. Housebreaking will offer few problems. However, if left alone, frequently they will develop chewing problems or will chase around the apartment doing damage. Strenuous exercise before leaving these high-spirited dogs alone may help.

Teaching them the proper commands will not be difficult. Authority and firmness should be the rule. Give immediate praise when the dog obeys a command and be exuberant.

RHODESIAN RIDGEBACK

Positive characteristics. Members of this large, powerful breed function very well in guard work. They are very tough and make excellent guard dogs. They are aggressive, but not in a vicious sense.

Ridgebacks are very intelligent dogs. They play and exercise hard, they are well suited to either the country or the city, and their short coats require minimal grooming.

Negative characteristics. These dogs are very self-willed and are definitely not for elderly people. It takes a very strong, firm individual to command them. Women, as a rule, have a difficult time handling these dogs. They take advantage of any owner who does not enforce discipline or allows poor response to each command. They can be very stubborn when they want to be.

Specific training problems. Because these are extremely stubborn dogs, you must exercise patience when teaching the basic obedience commands. However, you must make them obey every command given. Once they have been trained, do not allow them to disobey. Firm corrections are the only way to achieve success. They must be made to obey the first time, every time. Give immediate praise when the dog obeys a command and be exuberant.

When they walk, they must be made to walk by your side, rather than pull ahead as they tend to do. Ridgebacks are aggressive toward other dogs. This problem must be dealt with the minute it happens. (See Chapter 15, "Problem Dogs.") The basic obedience course will help. The key to their training is complete control at all times.

SALUKI

Positive characteristics. Considering their size, Salukis are good with elderly people. They are even-tempered animals and make excellent house pets in the city or country. These are very quiet, exotic dogs.

Negative characteristics. Because they are independent and aloof, they are not good family dogs. They usually appeal more to rugged individuals who lead rather singular lives. These dogs are not extroverted and, consequently, appeal to a few special types of people. It is hard for the average family to relate to this exclusive, private type of animal.

Specific training problems. Salukis respond to training, but not as well as other breeds because they are nervous and high strung. Noises make them skittish. It is not advisable to train them near busy streets or noisy environments. A peaceful country setting is the optimum training place. Because of their nervousness, you must reassure them with affection and praise whenever they respond properly. Give immediate praise when the dog obeys a command and be exuberant. Do not hold back.

WHIPPET

Positive characteristics. These truly are racing dogs much like the Greyhound, only smaller. They are affectionate, intelligent animals capable of running thirty-five miles an hour. Although they are geared for high-speed racing, they make very good house pets. They will sit indoors in a quiet, graceful manner and add dignity and decor to any room. Because they bark at strangers, they make good watchdogs. However, they are gentle in nature.

Negative characteristics. Whippets are fragile. They are very sensitive to loud noises and get skittish on the street. They are not recommended for children. These delicate creatures are not outgoing and are not demonstrative in a family situation.

Specific training problems. It is almost impossible to teach them commands while outdoors. The outdoor noises are too frightening for them. They must be trained indoors, with no distraction. Be sure these dogs have been taught to obey each command before trying them outside.

Do not use a metal choke collar. We suggest a nylon or leather choke, and at that you should not be too hard with your corrections. Give immediate praise when the dog obeys a command and be exuberant. Training will require patience. If you are too hard on this breed they will not trust you and will become very nervous. Their problem is that they are babied too much and often not allowed outside, which results in a very nervous, frightened dog. It is advisable to take them outside as small puppies and get them used to strange noises.

Group III

Working Dogs

―――――◆―――――

ALASKAN MALAMUTE

Positive characteristics. These dogs are like teddy bears. They are large, furry playmates and enjoy the roughhouse treatment of children. Children have been known to ride them like horses. Although it is not recommended, the breed can take a lot of punishment. These are cold-weather dogs, and can stand being outside the house for many hours during the winter months. Their fur is so thick that they are capable of enduring the coldest temperature without feeling it. However, these big dogs adapt to apartment life very well. They do not require too much exercise and behave lethargically when indoors.

train. Many of them become aggressive. These dogs need the
Negative characteristics. Malamutes are long-coated and shed a great deal. They are very stubborn and difficult to

firm hand of a strong man. They tend to become dog fighters.

Specific training problems. Although a metal choke collar is required for a firm correction, do not leave it on all the time. It will wear away the fur around the animal's neck.

Malamutes will housebreak satisfactorily if they are walked often and watched carefully during the training period. Obedience training must begin at an early age. These are stubborn dogs and not inclined to please their masters. They will constantly test you to see how much they can get away with. Give immediate praise when a command is obeyed and be exuberant.

If they are not trained properly they will become aggressive. They must not be hit, punished, or bombarded with "No."

There have been several cases where Malamutes have turned on their masters. It is not because they are a vicious breed, but rather because their owners believed a large dog requires harsh punishments.

"Heeling" is one of the most important lessons for these dogs. They grow to ninety or one hundred pounds and can pull you down the street. Be firm and demanding with them at an early age. "Come When Called" off-leash presents a problem. At times they refuse to respond. This command should be emphasized at all times.

Be very firm with them and make them obey as quickly as possible. Do not tolerate a refusal to respond to any command. Firm corrections are needed. The key to training these dogs is to start when they are very young.

BERNESE MOUNTAIN DOG

Positive characteristics. These are wonderful house and apartment dogs. They are very good with children. They have no special medical problems. They have excellent appetites, and live long, normal lives. These ancient Swiss aristocrats are extremely gentle and have even temperaments. Bernese Mountain Dogs are all-weather animals and require a minimum of grooming care. They are very loyal and focus their affections exclusively on their own families.

Negative characteristics. None.

Specific training problems. This is a very sensitive breed. Be patient and gentle in all training commands. Too many hard corrections will make the dog jerk shy.

When using a metal choke collar, do not leave it on the animal for long periods of time. It can wear away the long fur around the neck.

Give immediate praise when a command is obeyed and be exuberant.

BOUVIER DES FLANDRES

Positive characteristics. These large, shaggy animals are fine guard dogs and make excellent house pets. They are open with children and adore family life. Bouviers des Flandres are eager to please and learn quickly. They respond to training better than most breeds. They are in a class with the German Shepherd and the Standard Poodle as ideal domestic pets. They have even temperaments and are exceptionally gentle and loving.

Negative characteristics. The only negative factor is that their long-haired coats require a great deal of grooming which must not be put off. There was a case where a dog had to have his entire coat shaved because of the owner's neglect.

Specific training problems. None. If you show this dog what to do, he will do it. Give immediate praise when he obeys a command and be exuberant.

BOXER

Positive characteristics. Part of the great appeal of this breed is its wonderful facial formation. The sloping jowls and wrinkled cheeks create the most fascinating and heart-warming expressions. These dogs have such open, expressive features that you can tell what they are about to do before they do it. They are excellent dogs for children. They are powerful and can survive a child's play with great ease. Once they have been trained they respond very quickly when a command is given. There is very little grooming required for their short coats. They are sturdy and hearty and have good appetites.

Negative characteristics. The temperaments of Boxers vary from gentle to nervous to aggressive. It all depends on the bloodlines of the individual animal. Be sure of the breeder and the progenitors of the dog before making a purchase. This is one of the breeds that has been hurt by commercialization and inbreeding. Don't be afraid to ask questions or to ask to meet the puppy's dam and sire.

Specific training problems. Boxers are sensitive to corrections. They are also stubborn, which makes training difficult. The younger the dog, the better he will respond to obedience training. Once they reach six months or more, they are going to be set in their ways and offer great resistance to training. Teaching "Down" will be the most difficult command. They do not want to respond to it. Take your time with this command and spread it out over a long period.

Housebreaking will not be a difficult problem if it is started at a very early age.

Wait two seconds after the dog obeys a command to give him praise and be exuberant.

BULLMASTIFF

Positive characteristics. Bullmastiffs are solid-looking brutes that combine size, strength, and even temperaments. They are, in their own way, beautiful dogs. They were originally bred in England as a nonvicious attack dog for controlling poachers on large estates.

However, these are easygoing dogs and make excellent pets for elderly people. Regardless of their size, they are easy to handle. They are good with children and adapt to apartment life very well. They are also very good in the country. Members of this breed make fine guard dogs. They are gentle, alert, and very responsive to training. When kept indoors they are lethargic and sleep much of the time.

Negative characteristics. Because they are so large, they can be a problem if they become too protective as guard dogs. If economy is a consideration, then you must understand the expense involved in feeding these large, hungry animals.

Specific training problems. Training should begin when the dog is very young. Some of them can be stubborn, but this can be overcome in early training before it develops into a mature characteristic. The hardest command will be "Down." But here, too, if the training begins early in the dog's life it will not be a major problem.

Give immediate praise when a command is obeyed and be exuberant.

COLLIE

Positive characteristics. Most Collies live up to their reputation for beautiful temperaments. Naturally, the Collie's public image comes from the many many years of television's favorite dog, Lassie. Because of the Lassie TV series we tend to think of the Collie as a free spirit, roaming the countryside, running and walking great distances. That image is true if the animal is a country dog and allowed to roam around without being kept on-leash. However, the Collie is an excellent city dog, adaptable to apartment living, and not in dire need of much exercise.

Collies are easygoing and get comfortable in one area and stay there. They respond to training very well, obviously. They are wonderful with children and develop lasting relationships. So far, the breeding of Collies has been very responsible, producing a stable, even-tempered, responsive animal. Because they are not too high spirited and are not hard to handle, they make excellent pets for elderly people.

Negative characteristics. Collies are stubborn dogs to train. This opinion, however, is based on experience in training older Collies. They are more willing students when they are puppies. If training is put off they tend to develop aggressive traits (especially if they were ever hit) such as growling, nipping, or even biting. Some of them have turned on their masters.

Specific training problems. You must not leave a metal choke collar on the dog for any great length of time. It will wear away the fur around his neck. A leather choke collar is preferable.

Some Collies develop bad chewing habits when they are left alone. Make sure you are very patient with these dogs and never abuse them. You will create complex behavioral problems if you are too harsh or if you overjerk them. If the dog is too frisky and outgoing before a training session, simply calm him down in a soothing manner. You must use a soft touch. Give immediate praise when the dog obeys a command and be exuberant.

DOBERMAN PINSCHER

Positive characteristics. This breed is endowed with a tremendous willingness to please. Dobermans make formidable adversaries as guard dogs but are also fine companions who do very well with children. Contrary to their bad press, it is not true that they are vicious curs who will turn on their masters. It is only when beaten or abused that members of this breed have used their strength and biting power on their owners.

These dogs have never endeared themselves to anyone who has met them in the execution of their watchdog duties. These unusual animals offer the unique combination of love and protection for their families. In training they will respond to a basic obedience course better, quicker, and with more grace than any other breed. Dobermans have been bred and trained in several ways for various purposes. For example, the companion Doberman is ideal as a house pet and as a psychological deterrent against would-be assailants. There are also protective Dobermans, guard Dobermans, and attack Dobermans. As a unique member of the dog world, the Doberman has proven himself to be a loyal, faithful, and affectionate companion.

Negative characteristics. The negative aspects of these animals result from the breeding of each individual dog. Negative traits are common in Dobermans that have been bred from a line of high-strung and nervous dogs. It is important to examine a Doberman's pedigree before making a purchase. Seeing the dam and sire will help. If the dog is extremely sensitive he will require extra handling around strangers, in cars, and in new environments. Because of his protective nature, he can be regarded as vicious if he senses an impending attack on either himself or any member of his family. This, however, is often regarded as a positive trait.

Dobermans have a very low tolerance for overly strict discipline or abusive treatment. No one other than the immediate family can handle them. In many cases the master is the only one who can give a command. Unless the dog has been bred as a moderate-tempered animal, he must be introduced to strangers, and he will have nothing to do with them in any case. He will merely accept those strangers his master accepts. Often the dog's sensitivity causes nervousness and out of this can come shyness or over-aggressiveness.

It is very important to know why you want this breed. Be absolutely clear about the dog's tasks. They will greatly affect the kind of Doberman to purchase.

Specific training problems. It is important to know your Doberman's temperament. Is he easygoing, friendly, unafraid of noises, crowded areas, other people? If so, he can be trained in exactly the same way you would train most other breeds. A highly sensitive Doberman should be in the hands of a professional dog trainer.

The only difference in technique for the even-tempered Doberman is that the corrective jerk should not be too firm. These dogs are quick to learn and will understand in five minutes what it may take thirty minutes for other breeds to learn. Give immediate praise when a command is obeyed and be exuberant. This is important if they are to keep their good temperaments. They must never be made to feel that they are being punished. The keynote here is to maintain a light touch. Because of their extreme sensitivity they must not be shouted at or handled with abusive authority.

These dogs will not want to "Stay" in the "Sit" position for too long. Use a longer leash and keep praising the dog every moment he stays in position.

The "Down" and "Down-Stay" will require a little more time than usual for this breed. They must be introduced to these commands very gently.

With this breed conduct shorter but more frequent training sessions—two or three times a day are ideal. Dobermans must not be rushed into each command. If this time span is observed the results will be truly rewarding. It must be emphasized that affection and praise are quite necessary. However, a firm "No" must always be applied with each correction. Dobermans will respond to it better than most dogs. They must be taught that you are the boss and totally in control of the situation. If you are afraid of them they will know it immediately and use it as an advantage against you.

The guidelines for Dobermans are:

1. Do not abuse them.
2. Do not pamper them.
3. Make them feel that they are part of the family.

    4. Do not display fear because they will react to it.
    5. Treat them with kindness, praise, and affection.

GERMAN SHEPHERD DOG

Positive characteristics: This is the smartest breed of dog ever trained by Matthew Margolis. There is no dog more willing to learn and to respond to all phases of training. They represent everything a good, all-around dog should be. They are used for the blind, for guard work, for narcotic detection, and, at the same time, make a truly great house pet. Anyone can own a German Shepherd Dog. They are wonderful with children and elderly people. They are good in the city and the country. They are healthy eaters and live to a ripe old age. They can adapt to any environment.

Negative characteristics. These dogs are inordinate shedders. They shed their coats continuously.

    Because they are so popular, an inbreeding problem has developed over the years. Hip Dysplasia, a hereditary disease, seems to attack Shepherds more than other large breeds. This disease, in oversimplified terms, is a congenital dislocation of the hip socket and often cannot be detected until the animal is past eight months. Recent medical studies have indicated that overfeeding a Shepherd puppy can be a cause of Hip Dysplasia. Before purchasing a German Shepherd Dog it is important to discuss the animal's bloodlines with the breeder. If there is any evidence of Hip Dysplasia in the animal's background *do not buy it.* There is nothing more heartbreaking than living with a dog, any dog, for eight or ten months only to have him destroyed or undergo major surgery because of this painfully mortal illness. This is a grim consideration in choosing a German Shepherd Dog. Otherwise, there are no other negative aspects to the breed.

    There are many stories about Shepherds turning on their masters. Any dog that can be trained to lead the blind cannot be born with a vicious trait. No animal will remain even tempered if he is yelled at, hit, or beaten, which remains true for Shepherds, Dobermans, Collies, or Dachshunds. It is important to note that some animals have been purposely made vicious by their foolish owners.

Specific training problems. Give these animals every chance to learn, reward them with praise, make training a lot of fun, and you will have no problems with the obedience course in the first part of this book. Give immediate praise when the dog obeys a command and be exuberant.

GREAT DANE

Positive characteristics. There are many positive features attributable to the Great Dane. These are fine city and country dogs. Despite their size, they adapt very well to apartment living. Because of their size, they are very lethargic. Consequently, a small apartment does not represent a stifling existence. It is not cruel or unjust to keep a Dane in the city. They are wonderful with children. Their largeness is often overwhelming when they run and jump but their bounciness is always in the spirit of play. They are easygoing dogs with gentle natures. Because of their short coats they are easy to groom. Danes can be used in guard work.

Negative characteristics. There are some medical problems with this breed. Some specimens develop a swelling or soreness around the knees. These swellings are usually filled with water and other fluids. Because they are big-boned animals, they sometimes develop bone disorders and severe callouses. Consult a veterinarian for more details.

The medical history of the animal and his progenitors should be investigated before making a purchase. They are large eaters; one cannot be economy-minded and own a Great Dane.

Specific training problems. Great Danes should be housebroken at three months and obedience-trained at four months.

They are very sensitive dogs and require gentle handling. Too much jerking will make them shy and skittish. Give immediate praise when they obey a command and be exuberant. They should be exposed to traffic, noise, and strangers as young puppies.

These dogs are leaners. For whatever the reason, they like to lean on those closest to them. This can be a problem when they weigh 250 pounds. Decide early whether they are to be allowed this habit or not. Once you indulge it, they are going to be stubborn about breaking the habit. The same applies to jumping on the furniture. It's cute when they are puppies but very disturbing when they reach full size. These are wonderful dogs to own and offer very few training problems.

NEWFOUNDLAND

Positive characteristics. These outgoing dogs are among the finest-tempered, most responsive dogs in existence. They are lovable, affectionate, and very good with children. They will tolerate the abuse that children notoriously dish out. Newfoundlands love to play. They will never react with anger or snappishness to overexuberant children. They are wonderful family dogs and they thrive in the country. Their coats are very thick so they can take the coldest weather with ease and pleasure. In the city they adjust to apartment life with no difficulty because they are lethargic indoors. Most oversized dogs would rather spend the day sleeping or staying put in one place than running and jumping like many of the smaller, restless breeds. For this reason they make excellent pets for elderly people. They are companion, guard, playmate, and loyal friend combined in one magnificent dog.

Negative characteristics. These are very large dogs and require large amounts of food. They are not for the economy-minded. Although well suited for city living, they are not practical in a tiny apartment.

Specific training problems. You cannot be hard on Newfoundlands when training them. They are very sensitive and will become shy and skittish if jerked excessively. Although their great size demands a metal choke collar for training, it should be removed immediately after each session. The metal choke collar will wear the fur away from long-haired dogs.

When teaching the "Heel" or any basic command, take the time to show this breed what to do even if it takes a lot of repetition. It is better to repeat the teaching process than administer too many corrective jerks. Because they are so large does not necessarily mean they require hard correction. Easy correction is suggested because of their great sensitivity. However, this breed is very willing to please and will make hard corrections unnecessary. Give immediate praise when they obey a command and be exuberant.

Commands such as "Sit" and "Down" will take longer to teach. Eventually, they will respond properly. Be patient. Give them time to respond and then lavish a great deal of praise on them. The keynote to training this breed is to give them a lot of love and affection.

OLD ENGLISH SHEEPDOG

Positive characteristics. This breed has become popular because of its unique, furry appearance. These dogs seem to be stuffed animals come to life. The American Kennel Club standard indicates that their coats should be profuse but not excessive. However, it has become fashionable to promote the excessive coat look. Television advertising has, of late, recognized the visual appeal of the breed and uses it in many dog food commercials.

Sheepdogs have good temperaments and are ideal with children. Although they are irresistible as puppies, they become even more appealing as adults and add a woolly beauty to any household. Like many other breeds, they adjust well to city and country life. Because they are so strong, they can take the roughhouse play of children without getting hurt. These sturdy dogs can take a good strong correction and will offer few problems in an apartment.

Negative characteristics. Because of inbreeding, Old English Sheepdogs are sometimes nervous, aggressive, and stubborn. If they have been hit they are capable of having bad tempers and might even be vicious. In some cases both bad breeding and bad handling have conspired to create a very bad specimen. Because these dogs have become so commercialized, the breeding selection has been poor. Many specimens are bred without regard to weeding out the temperamentally unfit. The only safeguard is to become familiar with the animal's progenitors. Do not hesitate to ask questions about the dog's bloodline.

In reference to the animal's handling, it is common sense that an abused dog is eventually going to strike back out of fear and distrust. The answer is obvious. Never hit your dog.

Another negative factor is the required grooming, especially if you maintain that excessive, shaggy look. They do not have that marvelous look after one week of neglect. The fur becomes matted, soiled, dried, and hopelessly tangled. If they are not kept up every day they will eventually have to be completely shaved so that the fur will get another chance. It is costly to have these dogs groomed by professionals. Unless you can afford the cost of a professional groomer, you must be prepared to take on this daily task yourself. These excitable dogs are too difficult for elderly people to handle.

Specific training problems. This is a very stubborn breed and requires great firmness. Training should not begin until they are at least five or six months old. They do not mature until they are at least sixteen months old, thus making early training pointless. This only applies to obedience training. Housebreaking should begin at a very young age.

Do not use a metal choke collar at any time. The heavy metal will wear away the fur around the neck.

Almost every command in the obedience course will result in a struggle between you and the dog. This is especially true of "Down" and "Heel." These two commands should be emphasized. Give immediate praise when a command is obeyed but use a subdued tone of voice.

Sheepdogs should never be allowed off-leash; off-leash training is not recommended for this breed. When purchasing a Sheepdog, understand that it is going to take a lot of work to train him.

PULI

Positive characteristics. Sometimes known as the Hungarian Sheepdog, this breed offers an unusual feature. There are many persons who desire a dog that can tolerate a lot of roughhouse play, but at the same time do not want an oversized animal. These dogs fill that need. They are medium-sized dogs and are not fragile. Both dog and child can play for hours without hurting each other. They are also very responsive to training. Pulis make wonderful watchdogs. They are very protective of their families and demonstrate proper aggressiveness when necessary. Apartment life offers no hardship or difficulty for the Puli. They do not run around wildly or need excessive exercise.

Negative characteristics. Pulis can be too aggressive, almost to the point of viciousness. They are nervous and high-strung animals and are not recommended for elderly people. Occasionally you will find a specimen that is not good with children at all. The best way to purchase one is to deal with a reputable breeder and investigate the animal's bloodline for behavioral traits. When not from good bloodlines, Pulis are difficult dogs to own.

Specific training problems. Even a well-bred Puli is going to be stubborn. If the animal comes from poor bloodlines he may prove to be too nasty to live with. Training must start early in life, and the techniques of fear and punishment will irreparably damage their personalities. If they are hit they will become aggressive and, perhaps, biters as well. Give immediate praise when they obey a command but use a subdued tone of voice.

ROTTWEILER

Positive characteristics. These animals are among the finest guard dogs in the world. They have been bred especially for this work and have proven to be extremely effective. Family life suits them. They have even temperaments and are excellent with children. Because great care has been exercised in their breeding, they are capable of tolerating the rough play of children and even adults. These dogs are very responsive to training and highly tolerant of correction. If you need a very obedient dog and a good protector, then this is definitely the breed to buy. These powerful animals are majestic in carriage and beautiful in appearance.

Negative characteristics. Rottweilers are stubborn dogs. They require a very strong, dominant man's hand to maintain control. The stubbornness is the same as that of some of the hunting breeds.

Specific training problems. Because of their stubbornness, you are going to have to work very hard teaching each command. But the end result is well worth the trouble. They are very responsive to learning and ultimately obey perfectly. Getting through their stubbornness is the problem. They will fight you on each command. When being taught to "Heel," they will try to pull your arm out of its socket. The only answer is a very firm correction each time the dog fails to respond to your command. When practicing the "Heel" place the choke collar high on the animal's neck so that he will feel your corrections. Give immediate praise when they obey a command and be exuberant.

ST. BERNARD

Positive characteristics. The St. Bernard is the greatest bundle of fun in the world. They are phenomenal with children. These gentle dogs are very good in the country. They can endure the coldest temperatures for many hours. However, despite their size they are very good in the city and in an apartment. They are very responsive to obedience training. They want to please and can take a firm correction with no negative reaction. St. Bernards are loving, affectionate, and passive enough for elderly people to handle. They are not nervous or high strung, and because of their lethargic manner are well suited to small apartments.

Negative characteristics. St. Bernards slobber; saliva constantly foams at the corners of their mouths. It can be unappealing, depending on your tolerance for the more earthy qualities of animals. It could also be costly if you have fine furniture and carpeting. St. Bernards shed fur constantly and in large quantities. These huge dogs eat a great quantity of food daily so you should be aware of the cost.

Specific training problems. None. Teach them each command as outlined and they will respond very well. Some St. Bernards are more outgoing than others. The more lethargic the animal is the less willing he will be to please. The reverse is also true. When selecting a puppy try to choose the most outgoing of the litter. He will respond best to obedience training. No matter which puppy you get you will find him easy to housebreak. These are very clean animals. Do not overjerk them in your corrections. One firm correction should suffice for these willing pupils. Give immediate praise when they obey a command and be exuberant.

SAMOYED

Positive characteristics. Samoyeds are among the most beautiful dogs in the world. They have a pure, regal white fur broken only by a black nose and dark, almond-shaped eyes. They are good country dogs, especially in the winter. Their thick fur coats allow them to endure the coldest of climates. They respond well to training and are excellent with children. These rugged dogs weigh between fifty and sixty pounds and easily take the punishment of a child's play. They are easygoing dogs and respond well to the city because they do not require too much exercise.

Negative characteristics. These are very stubborn animals. They completely rebel against being left alone. This may account for their chewing problems. Housebreaking is difficult. As a matter of fact, teaching every command will be a battle between you and the dog. Eventually they will do what you want them to, but it will be a fight to reach that level of training.

Samoyeds require a great deal of grooming. They shed profusely and if their white fur is not cared for the beauty of the animal is lost.

Specific training problems. You must use a metal choke collar because of the need for firm correction. However, remove it immediately after each training session. The metal collar can wear the fur away. A leather choke collar is a good alternative.

The main training problems will be housebreaking and destructive chewing. If you are very patient with them, Samoyeds will ultimately respond well to training. You must be very firm if you are ever to get to that point. These dogs require the authority of a strong man during the training process. They are extremely stubborn. Punishment is no answer to their chewing problems. (See Chapters 13 and 14, "Puppy and Mature Problems" and "Mature Problems Only.")

Give immediate praise when they obey a command but use a subdued tone of voice.

SCHNAUZER, GIANT

Positive characteristics. Giant Schnauzers are one of the three types of Schnauzers. The Standard and Miniature are almost identical to the Giant except, of course, in size. Giant Schnauzers originated in Bavaria, where they were developed from the Standard to work with cattle. Since then they have been highly successful as guard dogs in Germany.

These are large, powerful dogs, and if they are going to be with elderly people, and they can, training is essential. These are good guard dogs and are great with children. They adjust well to country and city life and are not overexuberant. Giant Schnauzers have gentle natures and good, even temperaments. Because they are short-coated, little grooming is required.

Negative characteristics. The Giant Schnauzer is a very independent dog and is sometimes regarded as stubborn. For many owners this is the attraction and would, therefore, be discounted as a negative trait. It depends on one's personal attitude and taste.

Specific training problems. Adjust your teaching efforts to the temperament of your dog. If he is hypersensitive, then you must not be as hard on him as you normally would. If he is extra stubborn, then you must be extra firm. If he is typical of Giant Schnauzers, you need only show him what to do and he will do it with a minimum of correction. Give immediate praise when the dog obeys a command and be exuberant. These are beautiful animals to work with and they will respond very well to training.

SCHNAUZER (Standard and Miniature)

Positive characteristics. Both Standard and Miniature Schnauzers respond very well to training. Except for size, there is little difference between the two. They take corrections very well. Schnauzers are marvelous family dogs. They are very outgoing and affectionate and have a high tolerance for the rigors of a child's play.

These rugged animals are wonderful in the city. They are endowed with a positive kind of aggressiveness. They can be left alone for many hours without becoming lonely or bored. They are very responsive to affection and are eager to please. The more affection you give these dogs the more they will respond to you. Stemming from a work-dog tradition, Schnauzers are fearless and perceptive guard dogs.

Negative characteristics. Schnauzers have a stubborn streak. When they make up their minds to do something it is difficult to stop them. They are very strong-willed animals.

Specific training problems. For some unexplainable reason many Schnauzers have little desire to walk. They stubbornly stand fast and the more you pull the more they fight you. When you pull a dog you are actually choking him. Consequently, the more you choke him the more he's going to fight. If this happens, it is best to drop to your knees and coax the dog along, using playful entreaties and lavish praise. It will make a difference. Schnauzers require patience. Too much authority works against the training. You must show them what to do with patience and affection.

The toughest command to teach this breed will be "Down." Make sure they know "Sit," "Stay," and "Heel" before you teach "Down." However, they do respond to the other commands very well with no hesitation. Be firm with your corrections, but add a lot of praise immediately afterward. Give immediate praise when the dog obeys a command and be exuberant.

SHETLAND SHEEPDOG (*Sheltie*)

Positive characteristics. These miniature Collies are very loving, affectionate animals. They are excellent with elderly people because they are neither excitable nor aggressive. Quite the opposite, they are extremely gentle dogs. We suggest this breed for older children because Shelties are fragile and can be hurt by rambunctious six-year-olds. Shelties are ideal for small apartments. They take up very little space and are fairly docile. These dogs are also very good in the country. The peace and quiet of a rural environmint suit their sensitive temperaments.

Negative characteristics. Shetland Sheepdogs are nervous, hypertense animals, and tend toward shyness. They require extra loving and extra affection. These are not dogs that one can roughhouse with or even pat very hard. They are extremely sensitive. We do not recommend them as a family dog.

Specific training problems. Because of their extreme sensitivity they require tender loving care, especially during the training period. Do not use any form of a choke collar. Be gentle in all corrections; this applies to every command you teach them. This does not mean you shouldn't be firm when giving commands. Simply use a soft touch when making corrections and be sure to lavish them with praise. Give immediate priase when they obey a command and be very exuberant.

Shelties should be trained slowly. Take more time in teaching each command than in looking for immediate results. Otherwise, the result will be a very shy animal.

SIBERIAN HUSKY (*Siberian Chuchi*)

Positive characteristics. Increasing in popularity in the United States and Canada, these remarkably intelligent and gentle animals have the unique ability to adjust to any climate, any set of living circumstances. Siberians are dense-coated dogs capable of enduring the severest cold weather or the hottest temperature. They are a joy to behold in the country, especially in the snow, and yet live remarkably happy lives in the city. These beautiful dogs are usually silver and black (sometimes silver and red) and seem to wear a constant smile on their faces, owing to the unique shape of their lips which curve upward at the back of the mouth.

They are naturally gentle and friendly, rendering them useless as watchdogs but distinctive as warm, loving companions. Most silver- and black-colored Siberians have a black "mask" of fur around their eyes, which, when contrasted with the white fur of the head, gives them a menacing look that has often scared away a potential troublemaker. These North Country beauties are almost human in personality and engage in deep, meaningful relationships. They are the all-time pet for children. Sturdy and playful, they not only endure the rough play of children, they demand it. These dogs will go out of their way to sniff around a child, even a stranger, and entice him into playing. To hear the wolf-howl, or "singing," of a Siberian Husky is to be irresistibly drawn to him for life.

Negative characteristics. Siberians shed their thick coats several times a year and make a mess of expensive carpeting. It is impossible to brush up against one when you are in a dark suit without walking away with pounds of white fur on it.

These dogs sometimes develop into very picky eaters. If they do not have the company of another animal to eat with, or do not like what they are being served, they will go without food to the point of near-starvation. Huskies are extremely stubborn and hardheaded about having things their own way. For this reason they are not recommended for elderly people or for permissive men and women.

If not trained with great firmness and discipline, Huskies will pull your arm from its socket to get to another animal on the street or perhaps to some prospective playmate. They also do not tolerate being left alone for long periods of time. When this condition exists they will chew anything they can get to, including baseboards, curtains, and any number of household appliances. They are very high spirited and easily bored. Sometimes another animal is the only way to prevent their destructive behavior. Another dog or even a cat may do the trick.

Specific training problems. A metal choke collar is the only effective equipment for administering a correction. Bred for pulling heavy sleds, their collar and neck muscles are well developed and they will feel only the firmest correction. However, the metal collar must be removed immediately after each session as it tends to wear away the fur around the neck.

Occasionally an individual Husky has a hard time being housebroken. Huskies demand constant attention and many walks during the housebreaking period.

These dogs learn quickly and respond beautifully to training. However, they retain their self-willed independence and cannot be relied upon to obey every command even after the most arduous training program. They require frequent brush-up lessons to remind them who is boss and what is expected of them. They will test your authority every chance they can. Because they are so lovable and endearing, they will use all the wiles at their disposal to avoid obeying a command and to get their own way. Firmness and authority are the keynotes for controlling these dogs.

You must not allow yourself to indulge them when they violate their training. This will be the hardest thing about owning these magnificent childlike creatures. They will run, jump, or sing to distract you, and they too often succeed.

Wait one second after the dog obeys a command to give him praise and be exuberant.

Group IV

Terriers

AIREDALE TERRIER

Positive characteristics. In a physical sense, these are probably the best of the Terriers. They are tall, dignified animals with a rugged, beautiful stance. Airedales make excellent guard dogs. They are very protective of their homes and families and make a lot of noise whenever an intruder crosses the family threshold. They are fearless in any confrontation. They never back down. An almost perfect family dog, Airedales respond to training very well because of their even temperaments and quick responses. These remarkable dogs are wonderful in the country mostly because of their keen hunting abilities. On the other hand, they adapt well to city life and get along with children. To groom their rough wire coats, simply brush daily.

Negative characteristics. Like all Terrier breeds they are very stubborn, strong-willed, and independent. Unless they are taught obedience with a firm hand, they are not very enjoyable to have around. They get spoiled and try to dominate their households. Some are very finicky eaters.

Specific training problems. Airedales are very good house pets. They are always responsive during training and are very alert. They are willing to please. Most problems can be avoided if training begins early, if they are taught what to do, and if they are made to obey and not allowed to ignore any commands. Give immediate praise when they obey a command and be exuberant. If you allow a year or a year and a half to go by before training, you will have many difficult problems ahead of you.

BEDLINGTON TERRIER

Positive characteristics. This uncommon breed has a very unusual appearance. Its blue-gray coat (sometimes liver color) is curly on the head and face and forms a topknot which is indicative of the breed. To the novice, this dog might look like a lamb. These very lovable dogs are rarely seen outside the home of a true fancier or the show ring.

Bedlingtons afford their owners the opportunity to answer all manner of questions from many uninitiated admirers. Unlike other Terriers, Bedlingtons are not terribly aggressive or high spirited. They are very easygoing and ideal for city life. They are also well suited for elderly people and children.

Negative characteristics. Like all Terriers, the Bedlington has a stubborn quality. Whether this is negative depends on each owner's respective point of view.

Specific training problems. Because these dogs are stubborn and strong-willed, you must be firm in all corrections. However, exercise patience during the training period. Give the dog plenty of time to learn each command before initiating any corrections. Wait two seconds after the dog obeys a command to give him praise and be exuberant.

Bedlingtons will test you quite often, so you mustn't be afraid to correct them. They are very sturdy little dogs and can take any reasonable correction. The trick is not to over-jerk them.

BULL TERRIER

Positive characteristics. It is accepted as fact that the Bull Terrier was created by mating a Bulldog with the now-extinct White English Terrier. The Spanish Pointer was later introduced to the line, as was the all-white specimen, to create the breed as we see it today. There are those who compare this dog with figures on an Egyptian wall carving and others who liken it to a carved face on a white squash. (What's so lovable about a white squash?)

To those who really know the breed, these animals are

friendly, affectionate, and good-natured. And certainly to those who own them or have owned them, they are beautiful brutes. These lively dogs are marvelous with children and are well suited to apartment life. Because they are so frisky, they also make excellent country dogs. They are gentle dogs who have short coats and require very little grooming.

Negative characteristics. Not everyone is suited to owning a Bull Terrier. It is suggested that you learn more about the breed on a first-hand basis before deciding this is the dog for you. (General George Patton took a fancy to this breed during World War II.) They are stubborn, like all Terriers, but for many fanciers that is interpreted as independence and is therefore considered a positive characteristic.

Bull Terriers were originally bred for pit fighting when it was a gentleman's sport in nineteenth-century England. The instinct to fight still remains, even though the sport does not. These animals make excellent guard dogs. However, once they are trained for that purpose they become very deadly weapons, and that's something to consider before going into it.

Specific training problems. Although these dogs are willing to learn, they still have the stubborn streak that is indicative of all the Terriers. They will resist each command you try to teach. This stubbornness can only be overcome by patience and firmness. Take each command slowly, but let the dog know who is boss in the situation. Give immediate praise when they obey a command and be exuberant.

CAIRN TERRIER

Positive characteristics. These mighty little dogs were developed in Scotland and, despite their small size, were bred as fine hunters. Cairns have sporting instincts with a good ability for vermin killing. It was a Cairn Terrier that appeared in the motion picture *The Wizard of Oz* as Judy Garland's dog. They are lovable and very devoted animals. They relate well to children and elderly people. Cairn Terriers adapt well to both country and city life and make excellent house pets. Their wiry coats require very little grooming.

Negative characteristics. None.

Specific training problems. As with almost all Terrier breeds, they have that aggressive, stubborn quality that makes them tough, scrappy little animals. You must be firm. Four months old is not too early to start their training. Do not overjerk any dog that is very young. Be gentle and patient. Give immediate praise when they obey a command and be exuberant.

DANDIE DINMONT TERRIER

Positive characteristics. This unusual Terrier breed was given its name by Sir Walter Scott. In *Guy Mannering,* one of his romantic novels about Scotland, the character Dandie Dinmont kept six of these small Terriers. The novel's success in 1815 immortalized the breed as Dandie Dinmont's Terriers. The breed itself was first immortalized by Gainsborough in 1770 when he painted a beautiful specimen in his portrait of Henry, third Duke of Buccleuch. Once a favorite hunting dog in Scotland and England, Dandie Dinmonts retain all the qualities of an excellent family dog. Very yappy, they make good watchdogs. They are wonderful for children and elderly people, and are truly the perfect apartment-size dog.

Negative characteristics. None.

Specific training problems. These dogs can become stubborn if they are not trained at an early age. Four months old is not too early to start their training. Do not overjerk any dog that is very young. Be gentle and patient. Give immediate praise when they obey a command and be exuberant.

FOX TERRIER *(Wire and Smooth)*

Positive characteristics. These small dogs, among the most popular in the world, are very sturdy and respond to training very well. They are capable of accepting a correction without being ruffled. Fox Terriers are adaptable to the city and are very well suited for long walks. Once they have been trained they do not pull on the leash, are easy to control, and do not get skittish. Although they are spirited animals, they are very good for children and elderly people. They are compact and travel easily. Their outstanding characteristic is their outgoingness, their desire for love and affection. They require very little grooming.

Negative characteristics. Fox Terriers are constantly yapping. They are nervous, high strung, and at times aggressive. Almost a reflection of our time, they do not know how to relax. They seem to suffer from hypertension.

Specific training problems. Because these dogs are so small and affectionate, they become spoiled by being overindulged. Owners tend to pamper them to the point where training is useless. Once they are spoiled they become stubborn and strong-willed. You must maintain self-control with this breed. You must maintain discipline, especially during the training period. Do not use a choke collar. Either a leather or nylon collar will suffice. Corrections must be firm but not severe. A strong vocal correction with a gentle corrective jerk will do the job. Wait four or five seconds after the dog obeys a command to give him praise and use a subdued tone of voice. Chewing and housebreaking are the most difficult problems to solve. Begin training at an early age; three months is suggested.

KERRY BLUE TERRIER

Positive characteristics. Kerry Blue Terriers represent the paradox that exists in the world of purebred dogs. These rare and elegantly groomed creatures, seldom seen out of the show ring, come from circumstances far less chic than the dog arena. Originating from the mountainous regions of County Kerry, Ireland, Kerry Blues were used for sheep and cattle herding, retrieving, and for killing rats, badgers, and rabbits. And yet, today they are true expressions of status and elegance when seen in a large city.

Despite that, they make excellent companions and house pets. They take to elderly people very well and enjoy all the roughhouse play of children. Strong and protective, they make fine guard dogs. Kerry Blue Terriers possess matchless beauty in their blue-black, curly coats. Many women compare their fur to Persian lamb. They never shed.

Negative characteristics. They are one of the most stubborn of all the Terriers. Kerry Blues are also very aggressive toward other dogs. They are constant dog fighters and require a very strong hand. Only women who are willing to be firm at all times should consider this animal. Under no circumstances should this breed be indulged. They take great advantage of those who spoil them.

Specific training problems. This is one of those breeds that absolutely requires a choke collar. You must use the choke collar firmly on every command. They can take firm corrections and must be made to understand that you mean business. Give immediate praise when they obey a command and be exuberant.

Teaching "Down" will present the biggest problem. They do not want to respond to this command. Extra patience and extra time will be required. Spread the lessons out for this command. Two a day for a week are not excessive. Give as many lessons as necessary for the dog to learn the command and to respond to it properly. Be patient and firm. It is also suggested that you select a training site that has no distractions. It will make the task that much easier for you and the dog.

SCOTTISH TERRIER

Positive characteristics. Legend has it that the Scottish Terrier is the original breed from which all the Scottish and English Terriers descend. Although it cannot be proven conclusively, many owners of the breed will swear it is true. These staunch little dogs are very popular in the United States. One was seen in the White House during the long administration of Franklin Delano Roosevelt.

They are very affectionate and make excellent companions and house pets. They are good in the city and the country. Their compact size and even temperaments make them ideal for children and elderly people.

Negative characteristics. Scottish Terriers do not like being left alone, which can create problems for those who must go to work every day, leaving their dogs to their own devices. They also have a difficult time being housebroken. These dogs manifest the traditional Terrier stubbornness.

Specific training problems. Extra time and patience will be required during the housebreaking period. Scottish Terriers have to be watched constantly for indiscretions. The minute the dog begins to mess, you must startle him with the "throw can," say "No" in a firm voice, and take him outside immediately. Other than that, they are very responsive to training and have no special problems. Give immediate praise when they obey a command and be exuberant.

SEALYHAM TERRIER

Positive characteristics. It is hard to believe that the elegant dog we see in the show ring, the one with the long, silky white fur was originally bred to kill vermin. The Sealyham originated in Wales and is named after the estate of its first breeder. Developed from an obscure ancestry, Sealyhams became proficient at exterminating badgers, otters, and foxes. It is, no doubt, these beginnings that created the Sealyham's instinct for guard work. They are excellent watchdogs and very perceptive at determining friend from foe.

In the home they are second to none as loving, loyal pets. They respond to training very well and have a great willingness to please. Sealyhams make excellent pets for children. They have a great propensity for play and a physical stamina for the rough treatment of children. The Sealyham is a unique breed and not too commonly seen.

Negative characteristics. The only negative aspect of this breed is the one that is characteristic of all Terriers: stubbornness.

Specific training problems. The most difficult command to teach them is "Down." It will require extra effort, patience, and much praise. Reinforce every command you teach with great affection. If you merely apply the corrective jerk when things do not go well, you are going to have a terrible fight on your hands. Like most Terrier breeds, Sealyhams will test to see how much they can get away with. Be firm. Use a choke collar. However, remove the collar immediately after training sessions, otherwise their fur will wear away at the neck. Give immediate praise when they obey a command and be exuberant.

WEST HIGHLAND WHITE TERRIER

Positive characteristics. Many dog fanciers consider the West Highland the best of all the Terrier breeds. These little dogs are surely the model for those fancy stuffed dogs sold at exclusive toy stores. They are among the best dogs for apartment living. They are compact, yet rugged, high in intelligence, and faithful to the end. West Highlands, with their marvelous temperaments, are ideal for children and elderly people. They are gentle, responsive, and beautiful.

Negative characteristics. None.

Specific training problems. They do not have the typical stubborn quality indicative of most Terriers. You merely have to show them what to do and they will do it. Give immediate praise when they obey a command and be exuberant.

Group V

Toys

CHIHUAHUA

Positive characteristics. The most obvious fact about this very special breed is its size. These dogs are ideal for those who want as little dog as possible in their lives without giving up the notion entirely. They are tiny creatures with "apple-domed" heads, and they range from one to six pounds.

The smaller Chihuahuas will fit into a jacket pocket or a woman's handbag. These frail creatures were introduced to nondog fanciers in the United States by Xavier Cugat and his Latin American orchestra. In most of his films the popular band leader held the dog in his arms during his musical numbers. This helped make the breed fashionable. They may be the best house pets for elderly people owing to their size and ability to be easily controlled.

Negative characteristics. Probably the most negative aspect of this breed is learning to spell Chihuahua. Although they are affectionate, they do not warm up to more than one or two people. Because these tiny animals are so pampered and spoiled (they are carried everywhere), they become insecure and frightened of anything unfamiliar. This causes them to withdraw from everyone but their owners. Dogs very often express their fears through aggressiveness, and that sometimes is the case with Chihuahuas.

Specific training problems. They are very difficult to train. They are trainable up to five or six months old. After that it is not really worth the trouble. However, they rarely have need for some of the obedience commands such as "Heel."

Give immediate praise when they obey a command and be exuberant.

MALTESE

Positive characteristics. Of all the Toy breeds, the Maltese is probably the brightest, the most responsive, and the most beautiful. Originating on the Island of Malta, this breed has been known as the aristocrat of the canine world for twenty-eight centuries. Through ancient and modern history, the Maltese has been associated with the cultured, wealthy, and powerful. They are truly the princes and princesses of the dog world.

Their long silken coats are of the purest white fluffy fur. Although they are officially classified as Spaniels, they may have a touch of Terrier, judging from their instinct for hunting. Looking like delicate porcelain figurines, these graceful dogs prance from room to room with mercurial speed. Their tiny appearance is misleading, however. They are sturdy dogs with great stamina and hearty appetites. They are clean, refined, and faithful. They are wonderful for elderly people and ideally suited to apartment life. Known to the Phoenicians, the Greeks, and the Romans, these beautiful creatures are historically famous for their sweet temperaments.

Negative characteristics. Of all the breeds this one tends to be pampered and spoiled the most. Consequently, they become insecure and totally dependent on their masters. Grooming them is a big job. Their long white fur can be a nightmare to deal with if neglected for even the shortest period of time. Their coats get matted and their eyes stain the white face fur. There is a great deal of daily work involved in keeping this dog beautiful.

Specific training problems. Never use a choke collar with this breed. They are too delicate.

Housebreaking will be the biggest training problem. Because they are so small they are usually paper-trained. However, after a while they tend to have many indiscretions. If you change to housebreaking once the dog has been paper-trained, you will experience great difficulty. The only answer is to keep a watchful eye on the animal no matter which technique you use, and continue to implement the training until the problem is resolved. The best answer would be to select one kind of training and remain consistent to it.

Give immediate praise when they obey a command and be exuberant.

PEKINGESE

Positive characteristics. Like collectors of rare, Oriental art objects, the Pekingese owners love to expound on the many esoteric facts and fantasies surrounding this breed. For example, the oldest strains—which were bred by the Imperial Family of China, dating back to the Tang Dynasty—were kept pure, and the theft of one of the "sacred dogs" was punishable by death. The Pekingese of today, though descendants of Oriental royalty, are more common among American dog fanciers and pet owners than their progenitors were among Chinese peasants. These unusual-looking dogs make excellent house pets, and are very well suited to apartment living. They are good with children, though they are best for elderly people.

Negative characteristics. Their long, silky coats require a great deal of grooming. Be prepared to spend a lot of time with a brush in your hand. They have a strong stubborn streak and can be very noisy when a doorbell rings.

Specific training problems. Gentleness is the keynote to training this breed. You must never use a choke collar for them. Pekingese are very willing to learn, but they are sensitive and should not be jerked too hard. Give immediate praise when they obey a command and be exuberant. If you take the time to teach them the basic commands, you will always have a responsive, disciplined pet.

Because of their size, paper training is suggested rather than housebreaking.

POODLE (*Toy*)

Positive characteristics. The most obvious factor here is size. The Toy Poodle is the smallest of all the various Poodles. For many potential dog owners, size is the most important consideration. As the name implies, these are tiny animals and measure under ten inches at the shoulder. It is important to note that all Poodles are similar in every way, except size. (See "Poodle [Standard and Miniature]" listed in *Group VI: Nonsporting Dogs.*)

Poodles are very affectionate dogs and are excellent with elderly people. They are also good with children, but perhaps the larger ones are more capable of enduring their rough-house play. Poodles are the only dogs that do not affect those who have various allergies. These dogs are very gentle, loving animals and set the standard for all house pets. They are among the best dogs.

Negative characteristics. They are usually spoiled by their owners and become stubborn and yappy. They will bark at the least bit of disturbance and insist that things be done the way they want them. This only happens when they are treated like human babies.

Specific training problems. These animals require discipline and the obligation to obey all commands. If they are indulged like spoiled children they will never be trainable. The key-note to training Poodles is to treat them like animals, not children. However, you must not use a choke collar on Toy Poodles. They are simply too delicate. Give immediate praise when they obey a command and be exuberant.

PUG

Positive characteristics. Can a dog with a pushed-in face, small brutish body, and loose lines of flesh around the shoulders be considered beautiful? Ask any Pug owner. Pugs do not need coddling and have adapted to various working tasks not expected of a Toy breed. These dogs are affectionate in a quiet, dignified way. They are good in a brace because the tend to get along with other dogs. Many owners keep two. They adapt very well to the city and make wonderful family pets. They are short-coated and require very little grooming.

Negative characteristics. They suffer from a shortness of breath that often sounds like asthma. Because of their breathing difficulties, Pugs cannot be left alone in a closed car, even with the windows slightly open. They will suffocate. If you have occasion to travel frequently, this is not the dog for you.

Specific training problems. Never use a choke collar with this breed. Because of their breathing problem the training sessions must be very short. No lesson should last longer than five minutes and the dog must not be jerked very much. You may give two five-minute lessons within a one-hour period.

Do not train these dogs where there are distractions. The objective is to try to avoid as many corrections as possible. Be gentle and patient. Wait three seconds after the dog obeys a command to give him praise and use a subdued tone of voice.

SILKY TERRIER

Positive characteristics. The Silkys are very loving, affectionate, and outgoing dogs. They are true lap dogs, even though they have been used in their native Australia as workers, hunting rats and snakes. These compact animals are completely portable and travel well. They are also wonderful pets for small apartments. Silkys are small but very sturdy and capable of taking a great deal of abuse from children. They are ideal as an all-around family pet.

Negative characteristics. Like most Terriers, they have a stubborn streak. Housebreaking will be problematic. Their long silken coats bear constant care and grooming. Keeping the dog indoors is often the only solution to excessive grooming.

Specific training problems. Do not use a choke collar; use a leather or nylon collar and leash. These dogs can be excitable and consequently will be distracted very easily. Try to keep their attention. In the early phase of training use a quiet street or the privacy of your home. Once they learn the commands, you can work them outside where there are noises and strange people. Their stubborn quality must be met with firmness when they disobey. Wait two seconds after the dog obeys a command to give him praise and use a subdued tone of voice. Train them at an early age.

YORKSHIRE TERRIER

Positive characteristics. These diminutive aristocrats were developed as a breed late in the nineteenth century, but won early acceptance among the wealthy families of the Victorian era. Even today these spirited sprites appeal to the more fashion-minded pet owners and dog fanciers. "Yorkys" are very often kept as decorative lap dogs with no function other than raising the status of their owners. Nevertheless, Yorkshire Terriers are wonderful pets for children and elderly people. Because they are of the Terrier bloodlines, they are sturdy and have lots of spunk. They are equally at home in the country and the city. These dogs are extremely intelligent.

Negative characteristics. Yorkshire Terriers are difficult to housebreak. They manifest the same stubborn streak prevalent in most Terrier breeds. Because they have such long, silky coats, they require a great deal of grooming and constant watching. Many owners keep their "Yorkys" indoors to avoid extra grooming.

Specific training problems. They are aggressive and yappy. Their most difficult command is to "Heel." They dart from side to side and back and forth when being walked. You must be firm, demanding, and patient when teaching this command. Wait two seconds after the dog obeys a command to give him praise and use a subdued tone of voice.

It is recommended that you housebreak these dogs right at the start. Although they have difficulty being housebroken, they are even less reliable if paper-trained. They still have mishaps long after the training has ceased. During the housebreaking period they bear constant watching and many walks.

Do not use a choke collar; they are too delicate. Because they are stubborn, begin training at an early age. Be firm and patient. Most corrections should be vocal. Do not overjerk them. Because these dogs are so small and precocious, owners tend to spoil them. Once you do, they will never be trainable.

Group VI
Nonsporting Dogs

———————◆———————

BOSTON TERRIER

Positive characteristics. The Boston Terrier is one of the very few purebred dogs developed in the United States. Like most original Yankees, they were developed from English stock. They are a cross between the Bulldog and the English Terrier. In existence only since the Civil War, they have firmly secured a place for themselves in the world of purebred dogs. Though very powerful, Boston Terriers are small in size. They range from fifteen to twenty-five pounds.

These unusual-looking animals were used for many many years as the advertising symbol for Buster Brown Shoes. *"I'm Buster Brown, I live in a shoe. This is my dog Tige, he lives there, too."* Many children grew up with the Boston Terrier in mind as the ideal child's dog because of this ad slogan. Despite the slogan, it happens to be a fact. They are lovable animals and are wonderful for children. They are gentle but rugged dogs. They make excellent pets for elderly people, too. For those who are looking for a small, lively dog who does not require too much exercise, this is it.

Negative characteristics. Like most Terrier breeds, the Boston manifests that stubborn, aggressive streak. They are also extremely sensitive.

Specific training problems. These dogs have a difficult time being housebroken. They must be watched carefully and walked frequently. Because of their stubbornness, you must be firm and constant in making them obey. Take your time with each command and give them lavish praise whenever they respond correctly. Wait two seconds after the dog obeys a command to give him praise but be exuberant.

BULLDOG

Positive characteristics. Until 1835 this breed, like so many others in England, was used in cruel sports—in particular, bull baiting—and it created a tough, vicious animal. However, since their sporting days ended, Bulldogs have been bred for their stately physiques and sweet natures. There is probably not a gentler and more even-tempered dog in existence. Although the current specimens look nothing like their athletic progenitors, the original stamina, intelligence, and courage remain. These stocky brutes with their pushed-in faces, flapping jowls, and barrel-shaped bodies snort out their love and affection as they scare the pants off any potential attacker. Bulldogs are wonderful with children because of their very playful spirits. They can take all the punishment a child can dish out. Although they are delightful to watch in the country, they also make wonderful apartment dogs. They respond to training very well.

Negative characteristics. Most people pass up this breed because they do not like their physical appearance. The Bulldog looks mean (even though he isn't) and difficult to manage (which he is not). They do slobber, and for the fastidious housekeeper they are problematic. They also have a bit of a breathing problem.

Although this breed is the national dog of England, it does not possess the table manners of the very proper English people. Bulldogs are sloppy eaters and make the most intriguing sounds at dinnertime. If not trained early they can become unmanageable and problematic.

Specific training problems. Because of their great physical strength they are capable of taking the firmest correction. However, they are sensitive in nature and should not be overjerked. Bulldogs can be very stubborn and must be dealt with in a firm manner. Training should begin early. When it does, you will find them very willing students who will respond to vocal corrections and praise. Wait two seconds after the dog obeys a command to give him praise and do not be over-exuberant. They respond so well to training that it is almost effortless to teach them a new command. Once they understand that they must respond to you they will, and then training is a pleasurable occasion.

CHOW CHOW

Positive characteristics. These dogs were given their name in a very undignified manner. When trade was first opened with China, the term "Chow Chow" was pidgin English for any sort of gewgaw or bric-a-brac that filled the British ships' holds on their return to England. Among the imports were these rare and magnificent dogs that date back two thousand years in recorded Chinese history. They were lumped in with all the porcelain figurines and bamboo back-scratchers; the entire cargo was called "Chow Chow." Today the pidgin English term also graces the label of certain pickle jars, denoting a mixed assortment of sweet and sour dills.

Despite these indignities, the Chow has gained wide appeal throughout the Western world and is universally accepted as a fine watchdog. Faithful to Chinese traditions, these dogs quickly develop deep-rooted loyalties and strong protective emotions about their families. Because of this quality they make the ideal guard and companion dog. When groomed properly they are among the most striking and beautiful creatures in the dog world. Chows also respond very well to training. After you've owned one, fifteen years later you will want another.

Negative characteristics. Because these dogs are very aggressive, they are not ideal for everyone. Unless you match their aggressiveness with equal firmness they will end up dominating the household. These are remote and aloof animals who do not need or desire any undue expressions of emotion or play. Their blue-black tongues and set scowls do not always endear them to the average pet owner. They are not ideal for those who are purchasing their first dog. They require a true "dog person" to own them. By that is

meant a strong, firm individual who has owned several dogs
before.

Specific training problems. Chows require training at a young
age, when you have complete control of them. They are very
responsive dogs and learn anything you teach them. However,
they are stubborn and require a strong, firm hand. Give immediate praise when they obey a command and be exuberant.

DALMATION

Positive characteristics. Named after a province in Austria,
these dogs may represent the oldest unchanged breed in dog
history. Although many areas of the world claim these dogs
as an indigenous breed, they are generally accepted as Aus-
trian. This firehouse mascot has been nicknamed the English
Coach Dog, the Carriage Dog, the Plum Pudding Dog, and
the Spotted Dick. In the United States he is known as the
Firehouse Dog. These nicknames usually indicate the various
jobs and activities the dogs have been involved in.

   These spotted beauties make ideal pets in the city and the
country. They are obedient, responsive to training, and wonderful with children. They are capable of taking the pounding
of a child's play. They possess keen memories and are endowed with a willingness to please.

Negative characteristics. Dalmations shed a great deal and
are very stubborn dogs. One of the physical defects of the
breed is deafness. For some genetic reason many of them are
born this way. Before purchasing a puppy it is a good idea
to check for deafness. Because of so much inbreeding they
can be nasty, aggressive animals. Some poor specimens have
been known to bite children. Before making a purchase investigate the qualities of the prospective dog's dam and sire.

Specific training problems. Despite their stubbornness, they
are responsive and desire to please. They will require a slow,
firm approach to training. You will have to be a little more
forceful because of their excitability and nervousness. These
dogs require a strong, firm hand. Wait three seconds after
the dog obeys a command to give him praise and use a subdued tone of voice.

KEESHOND

Positive characteristics. Native to Holland, these "barge dogs" were largely unknown as a breed until the Dutch political leader of the nineteenth century Kees de Gyselaer used his own Keeshond as a political symbol of the lower and middle classes. The breed then went into obscurity for over a century, as did the party represented by Kees de Gyselaer. Keeshonds made their comeback in the early part of the twentieth century and were accepted as a pure breed in 1933.

These lively and intelligent animals make ideal companions in that they have no desire to leave their master's side. They are very furry in appearance and have wolflike coats. Keeshonds are very loving and affectionate. They are even tempered and responsive to training. They are not nervous or distracted by traffic and fare very well in city life. These rugged dogs get along very well with children and make ideal family pets.

Negative characteristics. They are stubborn, but not excessively so.

Specific training problems. Remove the choke collar immediately after each training session. It will wear away the fur around their necks.

Apply the basic training techniques, give them a lot of praise and affection, show them what to do, and they will respond beautifully to the training. Wait two seconds after the dog obeys a command to give him praise and do not be overexuberant.

LHASA APSO

Positive characteristics. The Lhasa Apso presents a rare combination of good qualities in a dog. They are small, hardy, rugged, frisky, intelligent, and very very beautiful. They are not lap dogs, even though they have become extremely fashionable in big-city apartments. They are ultra-elegant animals found among the chic and the wealthy.

These Tibetan dogs are loving and affectionate. Despite their small size, they are not fragile like so many of the Toy breeds. They can take a great deal of roughhouse play and for that reason are wonderful for children. These versatile dogs are very responsive to training and are completely portable. They can be taken anywhere on long trips with a minimum of inconvenience. Lhasa Apsos are very even tempered and fare well in the city.

Negative characteristics. If they are hit or overjerked when corrected, they will become aggressive and growl, snarl, or even bite. If they are hit they will bite whenever anyone tries to touch them. Grooming requires a very gentle hand or else the dog will get pinched when the brush is run through his long hard hair. Anything that pains the dog will make him aggressive. There is a great deal of grooming involved in keeping up this breed's appearance.

Specific training problems. If training begins at a young age and with a good deal of love and affection, you will have no problems. They must never be hit or corrected severely. If you are going to train a Lhasa Apso that is one year old or over, you must exercise great patience and take your time in teaching each command. Give immediate praise when they obey a command and be exuberant.

POODLE *(Standard and Miniature)*

Positive characteristics. Although this breed originated in Germany, it is considered the national dog of France. In France it is called *caniche.* There is little difference between the Standard and the Miniature Poodle except size. The Standard Poodle is fifteen inches or more at the shoulder and the Miniature is between ten and fifteen inches at the shoulder. The oversized Standard is informally called the Royal Standard.

These dogs are intelligent, frisky, dignified, and very elegant-looking. Some owners prefer their coats grown out, despite the fact that most adhere to show requirements which insist on the "Continental" clip or the "English Saddle" clip. Poodle fur does not affect a person with allergies.

In sheer numbers, the Poodle is probably the most popular breed in America. They are extremely intelligent, brilliant in training, and very desirous to please their masters.

Poodles are good family dogs. They get along very well both with children and with other animals. Many people own more than one. City life appeals to this breed. In major urban areas such as New York and Chicago, they represent status. There is no dog more cosmopolitan-looking than a poodle. They bring the boulevards of Paris with them no matter where they go.

Negative characteristics. Because they are so primped and pampered, they get spoiled by many of their owners. Otherwise, there are no negatives.

Specific training problems. None. These dogs are brilliant. Show them what to do and they will do it. Give immediate praise when they obey a command and be exuberant.

SHIH TZU

Positive characteristics. The exotic Chinese name Shih Tzu means lion dog. Certainly a cousin to the Tibetan Lhasa Apso, these long-haired Toys have only recently come into their own in the United States. They can quite literally serve as toys for careful, well-behaved children. They are excellent for elderly people. The Shih Tzu is a very fashionable dog appearing in the most expensive homes and apartments. Despite their size they can be enjoyed in the country where they will run and play vigorously. These warm and even-tempered animals are very responsive to training and are completely portable. Shih Tzus are the perfect traveling companion since they cause no traveling inconvenience.

Negative characteristics. They are difficult to housebreak.

Specific training problems. Never use a choke collar on these delicate animals.

Housebreaking is problematic. You must choose whether to housebreak or paper train them and then stick with your choice. During paper training you will find that from time to time they forget to use the paper. When that happens you must go back over the training and reinforce what they have already been taught.

Give immediate praise when they obey a command and be exuberant.

Index